DAPHNE DU MAURIER
Rebecca

Retold by Margaret Tarner

UPPER LEVEL

Founding Editor: John Milne

Macmillan Guided Readers provide a choice of enjoyable reading material for all learners of English. The series comprises three categories: MODERNS, CLASSICS and ORIGINALS. Macmillan **Classics** are retold versions of internationally recognised literature, published at four levels of grading—Beginner, Elementary, Intermediate and Upper. Readers at **Upper Level** are intended as an aid to students which will start them on the road to reading unsimplified books in the whole range of English literature. At the same time, the content and language of the Readers at **Upper Level** is carefully controlled with the following main features:

Information Control

As at other levels in the series, information vital to the development of a story is carefully presented in the text and then reinforced through the Points for Understanding section. Some background references may be unfamiliar to students, but these are explained in the text and in notes in the Glossary. Care is taken with pronoun reference.

Structure Control

Students can expect to meet those structures covered in any basic English course. Difficult structures, such as complex nominal groups and embedded clauses, are used sparingly. Clauses and phrases within sentences are carefully balanced and sentence length is limited to a maximum of four clauses in nearly all cases.

Vocabulary Control

At **Upper Level** there is a basic vocabulary of approximately 2200 words. At the same time, students are given the opportunity to meet new words, including some simple idiomatic and figurative English usages which are clearly explained in the Glossary.

Glossary

The Glossary at the back of this book is divided into sections. A number beside a word in the text, like this: ...[1], refers to a section of the Glossary. The words within each section are listed in alphabetical order. The page number beside a word in the Glossary refers to its first occurrence in the text.

Contents

The People in this Story

The narrator

Maxim de Winter

Frank Crawley

Favell

Mrs Danvers

Mrs Van Hopper

Introduction

The Dream of Manderley

*L*ast *night I dreamt I went to Manderley again. I stood in front of the iron gates at the beginning of the drive[1]. When I had first seen those gates, they had been open wide to welcome me. Now, in my dream, they were closed. Behind them, the drive went on to Manderley.*

In my dream, I was able to pass through the closed gates. I walked up the long winding[6] drive. The trees and flowers grew near to the drive and grass almost covered it. As I came to the last bend of the drive, I felt the old excitement. I was near to Manderley again. At last, I could see Manderley. The old house was as beautiful as ever.

It was moonlight in my dream. The pale light shone on the windows and grey stone walls of the old house. And in my dream I saw the sea. It was silent and smooth as glass. For a moment, the house seemed full of light. I thought that we were living there, happy and secure.

The moonlight shone more clearly. Now I saw that Manderley was an empty shell[6]. Only the grey stone walls remained standing. No one would ever live there again. We would never live there happily, Maxim and I. We would never live there free of Rebecca, free from thoughts of the past.

I woke up. Manderley was far away. Hard, bright sunlight shone into our bare hotel room. The long, empty day lay in front of us. Nothing much would happen. Nothing ever did. But we had a quiet peace, Maxim and I, that we had never known before. We did not talk about Manderley. I would never tell Maxim my dream. Manderley was no longer ours. It had been destroyed long ago by evil and hate.

We shall never go back to England. Even after nearly twenty years, the past is too near to us. We try to forget the fear and terror but sometimes we remember.

We are often bored in this dull little hotel. But people who are bored are not afraid. We read the English newspapers, but we never meet English people, thank God.

This hot little Mediterranean island is our home now. We shall never again feel the softer warmth of the English sun. We shall never again stand in the Happy Valley and smell the scent of its flowers. Here, the hard light of the sun shines on white walls. The trees are dusty. The sea is a clear blue.

We have lost a lot but I have at last grown up. I am very different from the shy, frightened girl who first went to Manderley. The fear and the terror made me a woman. A dull woman perhaps. But I am with my husband and he is all I need.

Sometimes I see a strange, lost look in Maxim's eyes. I know that his thoughts are far away. Then he sits quiet and still in his chair. After a time, he begins to talk. We talk about anything in order to forget the past. We have both known fear. We have both known pain and loneliness. That is all over now. Manderley has been destroyed. But we are still alive and we are both free.

1

I Meet Maxim de Winter

What would I be today if I had not gone to Monte Carlo with Mrs Van Hopper? I would have lived another life. I would have become a different person.

Mrs Van Hopper was not a pleasant woman. She loved to meet people who were rich and famous. Every summer, Mrs Van Hopper stayed at the Hotel Côte d'Azur, the biggest and most expensive hotel in Monte Carlo. Here, Mrs Van Hopper found out which well-known people were staying in the town. She always found an excuse to speak to them. Then, pretending to know them well, she asked her victims[6] rude questions in her loud American voice.

I was young and shy. I hated my life with Mrs Van Hopper, but she paid me a little money to be her companion. I was not exactly a servant and certainly not a friend.

We must have looked a strange pair as we walked into the hotel restaurant that day. Mrs Van Hopper walked in front of me on her high-heeled shoes. Her fat, heavy body swayed above her short fat legs. I followed slowly, my eyes looking down at the floor. With my straight hair and badly-fitting clothes I looked like an awkward[6] schoolgirl.

Mrs Van Hopper sat down at her usual table and stared at everyone in the restaurant.

'There isn't one well-known person here,' she said in her loud voice. 'There's no one I want to talk to.'

Mrs Van Hopper was very greedy. She ordered a large lunch for herself. Soon she was eating a large plateful of spaghetti. We ate in silence. The rich sauce ran down Mrs Van Hopper's chin. I looked away. Then I saw that a new guest was sitting down at the next table. Mrs Van Hopper saw him too. She put down her fork and stared at him hard. I saw an excited look come into her small eyes.

'It's Max de Winter,' she said to me. 'The man who owns Manderley. You must have heard of it – a beautiful old house in the west of England. He looks ill, doesn't he? His wife died suddenly last year. They say he's broken hearted[2].'

I felt sorry for de Winter already. He was Mrs Van Hopper's next victim. She finished her meal as quickly as possible. I knew what she was going to do.

There was a long seat in the hotel lounge, with a low table in front of it. The seat was between the restaurant and the main door of the hotel. Everyone who left the restaurant had to walk past this seat.

'I'll take my coffee in the lounge,' Mrs Van Hopper told the waiter, 'straight away.'

She turned to me, her eyes shining: 'Go upstairs and find that letter from my nephew, Billy. Bring it to me in the lounge and the photographs too. Billy met Max de Winter in London. Be quick.'

I went up to Mrs Van Hopper's rooms as slowly as I could. I hoped that de Winter would get away before I returned.

When I came back with the letter, Mrs Van Hopper was already on the seat in the lounge. De Winter was sitting next to her. He was a dark-haired, handsome man. His face was pale and his dark eyes had a sad, lost look. De Winter stood up politely as I gave Mrs Van Hopper her letter.

'Mr de Winter is having coffee with us. Go and ask the waiter for another cup,' Mrs Van Hopper told me.

'No, you are my guests,' said de Winter. He called the waiter.

In a moment, de Winter was sitting on a small chair and I was next to Mrs Van Hopper on the long seat.

'I recognized you at once,' Mrs Van Hopper said. 'I met my nephew's party, in London. But I don't suppose you reme an old woman like me?' And Mrs Van Hopper gave de Winter of her biggest smiles.

*Max de Winter's face was pale and his dark eyes had a sad,
lost look.*

'You are wrong, I could never forget you,' said de Winter in a cold, hard voice.

'Billy's on holiday now,' Mrs Van Hopper went on. 'He loves travelling. But if he had a home like Manderley, he would never leave it. People say that Manderley's one of the most beautiful houses in England. I wonder what you are doing here in Monte Carlo?'

For a few moments there was silence. Then de Winter spoke. 'Manderley was looking very lovely when I came away.' There was another silence. De Winter had not answered Mrs Van Hopper's question. She was not silent for long, of course. She started to tell de Winter all the unpleasant gossip[6] of Monte Carlo.

After his moment of rudeness, de Winter listened to her politely. I looked down at the floor and tried not to hear Mrs Van Hopper's loud voice. At last she had to stop. A waiter came up to her with a message. Mrs Van Hopper's dressmaker was waiting for her upstairs.

De Winter stood up at once. 'You mustn't keep your dressmaker waiting,' he said.

Mrs Van Hopper smiled. 'You must have a drink with me,' she said. 'Why not tomorrow evening? I'm having a few friends . . .'

'I'm sorry,' de Winter said quickly. 'I shall be away all day tomorrow. If you will excuse me . . .' He turned and walked out of the lounge.

'What a strange man Max de Winter is,' said Mrs Van Hopper when we were standing in the lift. 'He left so suddenly. But he is certainly an attractive man. By the way, dear, you were rather rude to him. You must look at people when they are speaking. You are not a child, you know.'

Mrs Van Hopper was soon busy with her dressmaker. I sat on a window seat, looking at the bright day outside. I could not go out. Some of Mrs Van Hopper's friends were coming to tea. They were fat, rude women like herself. My job was to talk to them, light their cigarettes and tidy the room after they had gone.

There was a knock on the door. A waiter came in with a note in his hand. 'Madame is in the bedroom,' I told him. But the note was for me. There were a few words in an unknown handwriting.

'Forgive me. I was very rude after lunch.' The note was not signed, but I knew it was from de Winter.

'Is there an answer?' the waiter asked me. I looked up. 'No. No answer,' I said.

After the waiter had gone, I put the note in my pocket. Mrs Van Hopper called me from her bedroom. I got up slowly, thinking about de Winter and about Manderley.

2

A Day Out Together

The following day, Mrs Van Hopper woke up with a sore throat and a high temperature. I rang up her doctor and he came round at once.

'You have flu, Madame,' the doctor told her. 'You won't get better unless you stay quietly in bed. Your heart isn't strong. You'll need a nurse to look after you. You must stay in bed for a week or two.'

'I'm sure I could look after Mrs Van Hopper,' I said. But the doctor said no. To my surprise, Mrs Van Hopper agreed with him. Monte Carlo had begun to bore her. She would enjoy staying in bed. She would enjoy giving orders to the nurse as well as to me.

The nurse soon arrived and I was no longer wanted. I went down to the restaurant by myself. I was glad to be alone. It was half an hour before our usual lunch-time. The restaurant was almost empty. I went to our usual table. Then I saw that de Winter was already at his table. It was too late for me to go back. I sat down

12

awkwardly trying not to look at him. As I picked up the menu, I knocked over the flowers on the table. The water went all over the cloth and ran down on to my skirt. The waiter was at the other end of the restaurant and saw nothing. In a moment, de Winter was standing by my chair.

'You can't sit here now,' he said. He called to the waiter who came up at once. 'Lay another place at my table,' de Winter said. 'This lady is lunching with me.'

'Oh no,' I said. 'I couldn't . . .'

'Why not?' he said. 'I want you to have lunch with me. I was going to ask you anyway. Come and sit down. You needn't talk if you don't want to.'

We ordered our food and sat for a time in a pleasant, easy silence.

'What's happened to your friend?' de Winter asked me. I told him about Mrs Van Hopper's illness.

'I'm sorry,' he said politely. 'You got my note, I suppose. It's very kind of you to lunch with me after my rudeness.'

'You were not rude,' I said. 'At least, she did not think you were. She is always so curious about anyone important.'

'Important? Why does she think that I'm important?' de Winter asked.

'I think it's because of Manderley,' I said. He did not answer. I felt that he did not want to talk about his home.

'Your friend is very different from you,' he said at last. 'And she's much older than you too. Is she a relation?'

'Mrs Van Hopper is not my friend,' I said. 'I work for her. I have to, I need the money. I have no family and there is nothing else I can do.'

De Winter asked me more questions about myself. I forgot my shyness. I told him about my father, who had been a painter. I talked about my mother and her great love for my father. When my father had died very suddenly, my mother had lived only a few weeks after him.

I suddenly realized that we had been sitting at the table for more than an hour. I began to apologize.

'But I've enjoyed this hour so much,' de Winter said. 'We are alike in some ways. We are both alone in the world. I have a sister, but that's all.'

'You forget,' I told him, 'that you have a home and I have none.'

'An empty house, even a very beautiful one, can be lonely,' de Winter said.

I thought for a moment that he was going to tell me about Manderley. But instead he said, 'Well, I suppose you have a holiday this afternoon. What are you going to do?'

I told him that I was going to do some sketching. I wanted to draw some of the old houses in a nearby town. The bus left at half past two.

'I'll drive you there in my car,' de Winter said. 'Go upstairs and get your coat.'

I got my things very quietly. I did not want Mrs Van Hopper to hear me. I ran down the stairs, holding my gloves in one hand. I felt excited and grown-up. I did not feel shy with de Winter. He enjoyed my company. He had asked me to go out with him in his car.

We soon reached the place where I wanted to sketch. But the wind was too strong – it blew the paper away. We got into the car again and drove on, up the steep mountain road. Then suddenly the road came to an end. De Winter stopped the car at the very edge. Far below us lay the sea. I felt cold and a little afraid.

'Do you know this place?' I said. 'Have you been here before?'

De Winter looked at me as though I were a stranger. He was lost in the past. There was a strange, faraway look on his face. He looked like a man walking in his sleep.

'It's getting late, shall we go home?' I said. Then he looked at me and smiled.

De Winter stopped the car at the very edge. Far below us lay the sea.

'I'm sorry,' he said. 'I should not have brought you up here. Yes, I have been here before, many years ago.'

Those years seemed to stretch between us. For the first time, I wished that I had not come.

De Winter turned the car carefully, and we drove down the twisting road again. The sun was setting now and the air was cold and clear.

Then, at last, he began to talk about Manderley. He did not talk about his life there, but about the house itself. He told me about the gardens and the flowers in the woods. He told me about the sea. It was so near that the sound of its waters could always be heard from the house. He told me about a little, secret valley close to the sea. This little valley, hidden away from the world, was full of the scent of flowers.

Then we were back in Monte Carlo. We drove slowly through the brightly lit streets towards the hotel. I took my gloves from the shelf of the car. There was a book there. I looked at it, trying to read the title.

'You can take the book and look at it, if you like,' de Winter said. I was glad and I held the book tightly in my hand. I wanted to have something of his now that our day was over.

'Out you get,' he said, 'I must put the car away. I won't see you tonight. I shall be out. But thank you for today.'

I walked slowly up the hotel steps. I felt like a child going home after a party. I thought of the long hours to bedtime. I could not meet Mrs Van Hopper and answer the endless questions. I went into the lounge and ordered tea.

The waiter brought me tea that was nearly cold. The sandwiches were dry, but I ate them without thinking. In my mind I was with Max de Winter at Manderley. If he loved his home so much, why had he left it?

I picked up the book he had given me. It was a book of poems. On the front page there was some writing – hard, clear writing in black ink:

"Max – from Rebecca, 17th May."

The name Rebecca stood out black and strong. The "R" was tall, much bigger than the other letters. I shut the book quickly. I remembered what Mrs Van Hopper had told me about de Winter's wife.

'It was dreadful,' she had said. 'Her death was in all the newspapers. They say he never talks about it, never says her name. Rebecca was drowned, you know, in the sea near Manderley.'

I stood up slowly, the book in my hand. I walked unhappily to the lift and back to Mrs Van Hopper.

3

In Love

I was twenty-one and de Winter was the first man I had ever loved. First love is not always happy. It can sometimes be like a terrible illness.

Mrs Van Hopper had been in bed for about ten days. She was bored now, and more bad tempered than usual. She asked me what I had been doing.

'You haven't got enough to do and so you are doing nothing,' she said unpleasantly. 'You never have any drawings to show me. When I ask you to do some shopping, you always forget something. You are getting lazy without me to watch you.'

I did not reply. I could not tell Mrs Van Hopper that every morning I drove with de Winter in his car. Every day I had lunch with him at his table.

I have forgotten the places we went to, but I have not forgotten the excitement of those mornings. I remember how I ran down the stairs because the lift was too slow. He was always waiting in his car, reading the paper. When he saw me, he would smile and say,

17

'Well, how is the companion this morning? Where would you like to go?'

If we had driven round in circles, I would not have cared. I was happy to sit next to him, to be alone with him. But the time always went too quickly. There was a clock in the car. I could not help looking at it as we drove along.

'If only we could keep our memories like scent in a bottle,' I said one day. 'And then we could open the bottle when we wanted to remember the moment again.'

'And what moment would you like to keep?' de Winter said with a smile.

'I'm not sure,' I began. Then I said quickly, 'I'd like to keep this moment and never forget it.'

De Winter laughed. I suddenly felt very young and very silly.

'I wish,' I said angrily, '. . . I wish I was a woman of about thirty-six. I wish I was wearing a lot of make-up and had expensive clothes.'

'You would not be in this car now if you were like that,' he said.

'Why do you ask me to come out in your car, day after day?' I said. 'I'm young, I know nothing. I am not an interesting person at all. You know all about me now. I have told you everything. But I know nothing about you, nothing – except that you live at Manderley and . . . and that your wife is dead.'

I had said the words, at last. Your wife. Your wife. He would never forgive me. I shall never drive with him again, I thought. He slowed down the car and we stopped by the side of the road. Then he turned to me and spoke.

'A little while ago, you said you wanted to keep your memories. For me, it is different. All my memories are unhappy. I want to forget them. Something happened a year ago that changed my whole life. I want to forget everything that happened to me before that time. That's why I came to Monte Carlo. If you had not been here, I would have left long ago. I ask you to drive with me because

18

I like you. I enjoy your company. If you don't believe me, you can get out of the car now.'

I sat very still. I could not speak. I could feel the tears coming into my eyes. 'I want to go home now,' I said.

Without a word, he started the car and we drove on. The tears began to run down my cheeks. Suddenly de Winter took my hand and kissed it. Then he gave me his handkerchief. I wiped my red eyes. I had never felt more alone.

'To hell[3] with this,' he said and put his arm round my shoulders. 'You are so young, I don't know how to speak to you. Forget everything I told you. Let's start again. My family always call me Maxim. I'd like you to call me that too.'

I smiled then, and he laughed back at me. The morning was happy again. The afternoon with Mrs Van Hopper did not matter. I could look forward to tomorrow morning and the morning after. I could call him Maxim. He had kissed me.

I had to play cards with Mrs Van Hopper that afternoon, but I was still happy. When we had finished our game, Mrs Van Hopper said, 'Tell me, is Max de Winter still in the hotel?'

'Yes. Yes, I think so. He comes into the restaurant sometimes,' I said.

Someone has told her, I thought. Someone has seen us together. I waited for her to ask more questions. But she did not.

'He's an attractive man,' she said, 'but not easy to know. I never saw his wife. People say she was very lovely. She was clever too, and always beautifully dressed, of course. Her death was very sudden. Everyone says he adored her.'

I did not answer. I was thinking about Rebecca – beautiful and clever. People could not forget her. Somehow, she and her beauty had not died.

In my bedroom was a book that Rebecca had held in her hands. His family called him Maxim. Rebecca had called him Max. I thought of the writing on that page. It was bold and full of life. Rebecca was all the things that I would never be. I thought

19

of all the letters Rebecca had written to her husband. They must have been full of the life they had shared.

I thought I could hear her voice calling him. She called him Max. It was her special name for him. And I had to call him Maxim.

4

I Leave Monte Carlo

Two days later, everything had changed. Mrs Van Hopper and I were ready to leave Monte Carlo. All the trunks and bags were packed. All the drawers and cupboards were empty.

Mrs Van Hopper had read a letter from her daughter at breakfast. 'Helen is sailing for New York on Saturday. Her child's ill. We are going too. I'm tired of living here. How would you like to see New York?'

The thought of leaving Monte Carlo and Maxim de Winter was a terrible one. My unhappiness must have shown on my face.

'What a strange child you are,' Mrs Van Hopper said. 'I can't understand you. I thought you didn't like Monte Carlo.'

'I've got used to it,' I said.

'Well, you'll have to get used to New York, that's all. We're going on the same boat as Helen. You'll have to arrange everything at once. Go down to the hotel office now. You will be too busy to feel unhappy.'

She laughed unpleasantly at my sad face. She walked over to the telephone. She wanted to tell everyone that she was leaving.

I went into the bathroom and locked the door. I wanted to be alone for a few minutes. My happiness was at an end. By tomorrow evening, I should be on the train. The train would carry me away from Maxim, mile by mile. He would be sitting in

20

the restaurant, reading perhaps and not thinking of me. Where would I say goodbye to him? In the lounge, with Mrs Van Hopper standing near? I was going and everything was over. We would say goodbye like two strangers.

Mrs Van Hopper knocked on the bathroom door.

'What are you doing in there?' she said. 'There's no time to dream this morning. There's too much to be done.'

I washed my face with cold water and came out of the bathroom at once. I spent the rest of the day packing and arranging the journey. In the evening, Mrs Van Hopper's friends came to say goodbye. We had dinner upstairs and Mrs Van Hopper went to bed early. I had not seen Maxim all day. I went down to the lounge at half past nine. A waiter saw me. He knew who I was looking for, of course.

'Mr de Winter is out this evening,' he told me. 'He will not be back before midnight.'

I walked slowly back up the stairs. Tomorrow would be too late. I should not be able to speak to him at all. That night I cried. My pillow was wet with tears. In the morning, my eyes were red and swollen.

'You haven't got a cold, have you?' said Mrs Van Hopper when she saw my face.

'No,' I said, 'I don't think so.' I tried not to look at her.

'I hate waiting around when everything is packed,' Mrs Van Hopper said bad-temperedly. 'We ought to have gone on the earlier train.' She looked at her watch. 'I think we could still catch it. Go down to the reception desk and ask. Hurry up.'

So my last morning was to be taken away from me. I would not see Maxim. Suddenly, I made up my mind. Instead of going down to the reception desk, I ran up the stairs. I knew the number of his room. I knocked on the door.

'Come in,' Maxim shouted. I opened the door. He was having breakfast at a small table in his sitting-room. I stood by the door, feeling silly and awkward.

'What do you want?' he said. 'Is something wrong?'

'I've come to say goodbye,' I said. 'We're going this morning. In about an hour. I thought I would not see you again.'

Maxim stared at me. 'Why didn't you tell me about this before?' he said.

'Mrs Van Hopper only decided to leave yesterday. Her daughter sails for New York on Saturday and we're going with her. I don't want to go. I'll hate New York.'

'Why go there, then?'

'I have to. I work for her, you know that. I can't afford to leave her.'

'Sit down,' he said. 'Have some coffee.'

'I haven't time,' I told him. 'I should be downstairs now.'

'Never mind about that, I've got to talk to you.'

I sat down at the table.

'So Mrs Van Hopper wants to go home,' said Maxim. 'So do I. She goes to New York and I go to Manderley. Which do you prefer? You can take your choice.'

'Please don't joke about it,' I said. 'I must say goodbye now.'

'I'm not joking,' said Maxim. 'Either you go to America with Mrs Van Hopper or you come home to Manderley with me.'

'Do you want a secretary?' I asked, not understanding him.

'No, I'm asking you to marry me, you little fool.'

I sat with my hands in my lap, watching him drink his coffee.

'You can't marry me,' I said at last. 'I'm different from you. I don't belong to your kind of world. I don't belong to a place like Manderley.'

'What do you know about Manderley?' Maxim said. 'I want you to marry me. Are you going to?'

I sat there, staring at him. I could not think clearly.

'The idea doesn't seem to please you,' Maxim said. 'I'm sorry, I thought you loved me.'

'I do love you,' I said, 'I do. I've been crying all night. I thought I would never see you again.'

When I said this, Maxim laughed and put his hand over mine.

'One day I'll remind you of those words. It's a pity you have to grow up,' he said.

Was Maxim laughing at me? Was it all a joke?

He saw the look on my face. 'I haven't done this very well, have I?' Maxim said. 'Men don't usually propose[6] at breakfast. But I'll take you to Venice for our honeymoon. We'll travel round Italy for a time. Then, in the spring, we'll go back to Manderley. I want to show you Manderley so much.'

Maxim wanted to show me Manderley. Suddenly I believed everything. I would be Maxim's wife. We would walk in the gardens of Manderley together. We would walk through that hidden valley to the sea. Mrs de Winter – I would be Mrs de Winter.

'Am I going to tell Mrs Van Hopper or are you?' said Maxim with a smile.

I had forgotten all about Mrs Van Hopper. 'You tell her,' I said. 'She'll be so angry.'

We got up from the table and walked out of the room together. Maxim took my hand. 'I'm forty-two,' he said. 'That must seem very old to you.'

'Oh, no,' I said. 'I don't like young men.' I was still afraid that Maxim would change his mind.

We came to the door of Mrs Van Hopper's rooms.

'I think I'll talk to her alone,' Maxim said. 'I'll tell her we are getting married very soon. We'll have a quiet wedding. Everything can be arranged in a few days.'

'Of course,' I said. 'I don't want a lot of fuss.'

I opened the door.

'Is that you?' called Mrs Van Hopper. 'Where have you been? What have you been doing all this time?'

I did not know whether to laugh or cry. Maxim walked towards the sitting-room.

'I'm afraid it's all my fault,' he said and then he shut the door. I went into my bedroom and waited.

23

I wondered what Maxim was saying to Mrs Van Hopper. Was he saying, 'I love her. I want to marry her at once.'?

Love. Maxim had not said anything to me about love. He had said we would get married. But he had not said that he loved me. He had loved Rebecca, of course. How could he love me, after her? I would be a companion for him. Someone to make him laugh perhaps.

The book of poems was beside me, on the bed. I opened it. I read again, 'Max, from Rebecca.' She was dead. But the writing still looked fresh and alive.

I took some scissors and cut the page out of the book. I tore up the page. I lit a match and set fire to the pieces. The paper twisted, blackened and turned to ashes. The letter "R" was the last to be burnt. Then the flame destroyed it. I washed my hands. I felt better, much better now.

As I stood there, the door opened and Maxim came in.

'Everything is all right,' he said. 'She could not speak at first. She was too surprised. Go in and talk to her. I'm going downstairs to arrange about her train. I don't want her to come to the wedding.'

Maxim was smiling, but he said nothing about being happy. He said nothing about love. I walked slowly into Mrs Van Hopper's bedroom. She was standing by the window, smoking a cigarette. She turned round and looked at me carefully.

'Well,' she said, 'you are more clever than I thought. How did you do it?'

I did not know what to say. Mrs Van Hopper was smiling, but there was no kindness in her smile. 'It was lucky for you that I was ill,' she said. 'You certainly made the most of your time. He tells me that he wants to marry you in a few days. Well, I can't stop you. He's much older than you, you know.'

'He's only forty-two,' I said. 'I know what I'm doing.' Mrs Van Hopper looked at me again with the same unpleasant smile.

'I hope you do. You won't find it easy to look after Manderley.

You haven't any experience and you're too shy. Max de Winter is very attractive, of course. But I think you're making a big mistake.'

I did not say anything. I was young and shy, I knew that. But I was going to be Mrs de Winter. I was going to live at Manderley. And I was going to make Maxim happy.

Mrs Van Hopper put out her cigarette. She walked slowly towards me.

'Of course,' she said, 'you know why he is marrying you, don't you? He's not in love with you. The truth is he's lonely by himself at Manderley. He can't live in that empty house without Rebecca. He's marrying you because he can't go on living there alone.'

5

I Come to Manderley

We came to Manderley early in May. It was the best time of year, before the heat of summer. When we left London, it was raining hard. I remember Maxim saying, 'This is London rain. The sun will be shining for you when we come to Manderley.'

He was right. Long before we reached Manderley, there was blue sky over our heads. I was glad to see the sun. I welcomed it as a sign of happiness.

'Feeling better?' said Maxim, looking at me. I smiled at him and took his hand. It was so easy for Maxim. He was going back to his own home. But for me, everything was new and strange. I was going to Manderley for the first time. And I was going there as the second wife of Maxim de Winter.

'Only two more miles,' said Maxim at last. 'Can you see those trees on the hill in front of us? Manderley is in the valley beyond those trees.'

I tried to smile but suddenly I felt lonely and afraid. I was like a child on her first day at school.

Turning a corner, we came to a crossroads and the beginning of a high wall.

'Here we are,' Maxim said. 'Manderley at last.' I could hear the excitement in his voice.

The road turned again. On the left, were two high iron gates and beside them a small lodge[1]. The gates were wide open for us. People were looking out of the windows of the lodge. They were looking at me. I sat back in my seat. I wanted to hide from their curious eyes.

'You mustn't mind if people stare at you,' Maxim said. 'They are all very interested in you. Don't worry. Be yourself[2] and everyone at Manderley will love you. Mrs Danvers looks after the house. She's been housekeeper here for years. Leave everything to her. She may be rather strange at first, but don't worry about that. She will soon get used to you.'

We were going along the drive now that led up to the house. The drive turned and twisted like a snake. The tall trees met over our heads. Only a little sunlight came through their thick branches. Everything was very quiet. On and on we went. Then suddenly the trees came to an end. The sun shone again. Beautiful high bushes covered with bright red flowers stood on either side of us.

We were not far from the house now. The drive widened. We turned the last corner and there was Manderley. The old house was perfect. It was built in a small hollow and its grey stones glowed in the sunlight. Smooth green lawns surrounded the house. Beyond the lawns were gardens and beyond the gardens, the sea.

Maxim drove up to the wide stone steps and stopped the car in front of them. At the top of the steps, a big door stood wide open. I saw that the hall beyond was full of people. I could see their faces, all turned towards us. I was suddenly shy and afraid again. 'What's the matter?' I said. 'Who are all those people?'

'I'm sorry,' Maxim said. 'This must be Mrs Danvers' idea. Everyone who works at Manderley is here. Don't look so frightened. You won't have to say anything. I'll do it all.'

An old man with a kind face came down the steps.

'Well, here we are, Frith,' said Maxim. 'Everyone well?'

'Yes, thank you, sir,' said Frith. 'We are all very glad to see you at home again. We hope you are well. And Madam too, of course.'

'Yes, we are both well, thank you, Frith. But we're tired from the drive and we want our tea. I didn't expect all these people.'

'Mrs Danvers' orders, sir,' said Frith.

'I thought so,' Maxim said. 'Come on,' he said to me. 'It won't take long and then you can have your tea in peace.'

We went together up the wide stone steps. Inside the open door, the servants stood in two lines. A tall, thin woman dressed in black came towards us. Her pale, thin face was hard. There was no welcome in her dark eyes. The hand she placed in mine was cold and heavy, like something dead.

'This is Mrs Danvers, our housekeeper,' said Maxim. The woman began to speak in a cold, lifeless voice. I remember nothing of what she said. I suppose she was welcoming me to Manderley. As I thanked her, Mrs Danvers looked at me with her hard, dark eyes. I dropped my gloves on the floor and Mrs Danvers picked them up with a twisted little smile on her lips. She could see that I was awkward and shy, and a little afraid of my new life at Manderley.

Maxim noticed nothing. He thanked Mrs Danvers quickly and took me into the library for tea. We were alone at last.

A dog ran up from the fireside to greet us. He went first to

An old man with a kind face came down the steps.

Maxim and then sat down beside me. I was glad of the dog's friendly welcome. The library was a large comfortable room. Its walls were covered with books from the floor to the ceiling. Comfortable chairs stood on either side of a great open fireplace. From its long windows I could see the lawns and beyond the lawns, the sea. There was a quiet peace in the room. It was a place for rest, for reading and for quiet thinking.

Tea was brought to us by Frith and a younger servant. There was a special table and a snow-white cloth to cover it. The teapot and kettle were of silver and the china was very fine. There were sandwiches, bread and butter and several kinds of cake. There was far too much food for two people. But this was the tea served at Manderley every day.

Maxim sat in a chair by the fire reading the letters that had been waiting for him. Now and again, he looked up at me and smiled. I leant back in my chair, drinking my tea and trying to feel at home. It was true. Manderley was my home now – my home and Maxim's. But somehow I still could not believe it.

My thoughts were interrupted by the opening of the door. It was Frith.

'Excuse me, Madam,' he said. 'Mrs Danvers asked if you would like to see your room.'

Maxim looked up from his letters. 'What do the rooms in the east wing[1] look like now?' he said.

'Very nice indeed, sir,' Frith replied. 'I think you will be very comfortable there.'

'Have you been making changes?' I asked.

'Oh, nothing much,' said Maxim. 'They have been getting the rooms in the east wing ready for us. There is a lovely view of the rose-garden from there. You go and make friends with Mrs Danvers. I'll come up later.'

I got up slowly and went out with Frith into the hall. I did not want to be alone with Mrs Danvers. The hall seemed very big, and my footsteps sounded very loud on the stone floor.

Mrs Danvers was standing at the top of the wide flight of stairs. Her dark eyes watched me as I walked slowly up the stairs towards her. 'I hope I haven't kept you waiting,' I said.

'It is my duty to wait for you, Madam,' Mrs Danvers said. 'I'm here to carry out your orders.'

She led me along a wide passage. We passed through doors and up and down wide stairs. At last Mrs Danvers opened a door leading into a small room. This room led into a large, light bedroom with wide windows. I went at once to a window and looked out. The rose-garden lay below me. Beyond the rose-garden, the smooth grass stretched to the woods.

'You can't see the sea from here,' I said, turning to Mrs Danvers.

'No, not from this wing,' she answered, 'and you can't hear it either. You would never know the sea was so near.'

Mrs Danvers spoke in a strange way, as though this was somehow important to her.

'I'm sorry about that; I like the sea,' I said. 'But this is a very charming room. I'm sure I shall be comfortable here.'

'Mr de Winter gave very careful orders in his letter about this room. The rooms here have been specially arranged for you.'

'Then this was not his bedroom before?'

'Oh, no, Madam. He has never used this room.'

There was silence. I did not know what to say. I wished Mrs Danvers would go away.

'I suppose you have been at Manderley for many years,' I said.

'Yes, Madam. I came here when the first Mrs de Winter was a bride[6].' Her voice was suddenly harsh. There was some colour in her pale face now. And for a moment I saw a look of hatred in her eyes.

'Mrs Danvers,' I heard myself saying, 'I hope we shall be friends. This sort of life is new to me. I do want to make Mr de Winter happy. I know I can leave the housekeeping to you. I shan't want to make any changes.'

'Very well,' she said. 'I hope you will be satisfied. I have been looking after the house for the past year. When the late[6] Mrs de Winter was alive, there were lots of parties and visitors, of course. She liked to look after everything herself.'

'I would rather leave it to you, Mrs Danvers,' I said. 'And I'm sure we'll be very comfortable in these rooms.'

'Mr de Winter said you would rather be on this side of the house. They used the rooms in the west wing[1] when Mrs de Winter was alive. The windows there look down to the sea.'

There was a sound outside the door and Mrs Danvers stopped talking. Maxim came into the room.

'Well, what do you think?' Maxim said to me. 'I hope you like the rooms. I think you've done very well, Mrs Danvers.'

'Thank you, sir,' she said. Then she turned and went quietly out of the room.

Maxim walked to the window. 'I love the rose-garden,' he said. 'There's something very quiet and peaceful about this room. How did you get[2] on with Mrs Danvers? She's a strange woman in many ways. I think that some of the young servants are afraid of her.'

'I expect we'll get on well when she knows me better,' I said. 'She may not like me at first, of course.'

'Not like you? Why shouldn't she like you?' said Maxim and he came across the room and kissed me gently.

'Let's forget about Mrs Danvers,' he said. 'Come along, and I'll show you Manderley.'

I felt happier as I walked through the house with Maxim. We looked at the pictures in the long gallery[1] and at most of the rooms downstairs. Maxim put his arm round my shoulder. I began to feel that Manderley really was my home.

After dinner, we sat in the library. The curtains were drawn[6] and more logs put on the fire. It was new for us to sit together quietly like this. In Italy we had walked about in the evenings, or gone for a drive. Maxim sat in the chair to the left of the fireplace.

We looked at the pictures in the long gallery.

He picked up the paper. He put a cushion behind his head and lit a cigarette.

This is what he always did, I thought. This is what he did before he knew me. It is what he has done every evening for years.

Maxim did not look at me. He went on reading his paper. He was comfortable, the master of his house. I poured myself another cup of coffee. I bent down to the dog and stroked its soft ears.

Suddenly I shivered as though a door had opened behind me. Someone else had sat in my chair. Someone else had poured coffee and stroked the dog. I was sitting in Rebecca's chair. I was leaning against Rebecca's cushion. The dog, Jasper, came to me because in the past he had come to Rebecca.

6

In the Morning-Room

Life at Manderley was very carefully planned. The same things happened at the same time every day. I remember our first morning there very clearly. I had slept well and came downstairs a little after nine o'clock. To my surprise, I found that Maxim had nearly finished his breakfast.

Maxim looked up at me and smiled.

'I always get up early here,' he said. 'Looking after Manderley takes a lot of my time. I work very hard. But you don't have to. Help yourself to anything you want.'

I remember the size of that breakfast. It was the normal Manderley breakfast, but far too much for two people. As I took an egg and some coffee, I wondered what happened to the food that was left. Would it be eaten or thrown away? I would never know of course. I would certainly be too afraid to ask.

'My sister, Beatrice, is coming over to lunch with her husband,' Maxim told me. 'She invited herself, of course. I suppose she wants to have a look at you.'

'They're coming today?' I said, feeling less happy than before.

'Yes, but she won't stay long. I think you'll like Beatrice. She believes in telling the truth. If she doesn't like you, she'll tell you so.'

Maxim stood up and lit a cigarette.

'I've so many things to do this morning. Why don't you go into the garden. You don't mind being alone, do you?'

'Of course not,' I said. 'I shall be perfectly happy.'

But I did not feel very happy as Maxim walked out of the room. I had thought we would spend our first morning at Manderley together.

I had thought that perhaps we would walk down to the sea, or sit under the great tree on the lawn.

I finished my breakfast alone. I left the dining-room and went into the library. The room was cold. The fire was laid, but not lit. I looked round for a box of matches, but I could not find one. I went across the hall and into the dining-room once more. Yes, there was a box of matches on the table. I picked it up. At that moment, Frith came into the room.

'Oh, Frith,' I said awkwardly, 'I could not find any matches. I thought I would light the fire in the library. It's rather cold in there.'

'The fire in the library is not usually lit until the afternoon, Madam,' he said. 'Mrs de Winter always used the morning-room before lunch. There is a good fire in there. Of course, I can give orders for the fire in the library to be lit.'

'Oh no,' I said. 'I'll go into the morning-room. Thank you, Frith.'

'Mrs de Winter always wrote her letters in the morning-room after breakfast. The house telephone is there too, if you want to talk to Mrs Danvers.'

'Thank you, Frith,' I said. I went into the hall again. I did not know which way to go. I could not tell Frith that I had never seen the morning-room. Maxim had not shown it to me the night before.

'You go through the drawing-room to the morning-room, Madam,' Frith said, watching me. 'Then turn to your left.'

'Thank you, Frith,' I said. I felt very stupid.

I found my way into the little morning-room. I was glad to see the dog, Jasper, there, sitting in front of the fire.

The morning-room was quite small and very different from the library. It was a woman's room, graceful and charming. Someone had chosen everything in this room with the greatest care. Each chair, each rug[1], each small ornament had been put there to make the room perfect.

Flowers filled the room, glowing blood-red flowers. They were the same flowers we had seen in the drive. A beautiful old writing-desk stood near the window. I went over and opened the desk carefully. Every drawer was labelled[6] and everything was in order. Inside one of the drawers was a flat leather book: 'Guests at Manderley'. I opened the book. The writing inside the book and the writing on the labels was the same. I had seen that tall sloping writing before. It was Rebecca's writing. This was Rebecca's desk. I sat down and opened the Guest Book. Every page was covered with the same writing.

I felt that Rebecca would come back into the room at any moment. The mistress of the house would come in and find me, a stranger, sitting at her desk.

Suddenly the telephone on the desk began to ring. My heart jumped. I picked up the phone. 'Who is it?' I said. 'Who do you want?'

'Mrs de Winter?' said a hard, deep voice, 'Mrs de Winter?'

My hand was shaking. 'I'm afraid you have made a mistake,' I said. 'Mrs de Winter has been dead for over a year.'

I suddenly realized what I had said.

A beautiful old writing-desk stood near the window.

'It's Mrs Danvers, Madam,' said the voice. 'I'm speaking to you on the house telephone.'

'I'm so sorry, Mrs Danvers,' I said. 'I didn't know what I was saying. I did not expect the telephone to ring.'

'I wondered if you had seen the menus for the day[1]. You will find the list on the desk beside you.'

I found the piece of paper and looked at it quickly.

'Yes, Mrs Danvers. Yes, very nice indeed.'

'I'm very sorry to have disturbed you, Madam.'

'You didn't disturb me at all. Thank you, Mrs Danvers,' I said.

I put down the phone and looked at the desk. I felt very stupid. Rebecca would not have answered like that. I thought of Rebecca sitting at that desk. Here she had chosen her guests and written letters to her friends. Who could I write to? I knew nobody. Then I thought of Mrs Van Hopper, far away in New York. I took a piece of paper and a pen.

'Dear Mrs Van Hopper,' I began. As I wrote I noticed my own handwriting for the first time. How weak and childish it was! It was like the writing of a schoolgirl.

7

'You Are So Very Different . . .'

When I heard the sound of a car in the drive, I stood up in sudden fear. Beatrice and her husband had arrived. They were earlier than I expected. And Maxim had not come back. I could not meet them by myself.

I ran quickly out of the morning-room. I took a door to the left. I was in a stone corridor[1]. A servant stared at me in surprise. I hurried up some stairs, hoping that I could find my way to my bedroom in the east wing. I could stay there until Maxim came back.

Somehow I lost my way. But I went on and came to a wide staircase. I went up it. All was quiet and dark. I was in a corridor with doors on either side. I walked on and at last I came to a long window. I looked out. Below me I could see green lawns and the sea. The sea was bright green, with white-topped waves. It was closer than I thought, much closer. I knew then that I had walked right round the house. I was standing in the corridor of the west wing. Yes, Mrs Danvers was right, you could hear the sea from here.

I was glad that my rooms were in the east wing. I loved the quiet beauty of the rose-garden. The sea was too near here. As I turned to go back to the stairs, I heard a door open behind me. Mrs Danvers stood there. We stared at one another for a moment without speaking.

'I lost my way,' I said, 'I was trying to find my room.'

'This is the west wing,' she said. 'Did you go into any of the rooms? If you wish to see them, please tell me. I could show them to you now.'

I shook my head. 'No, no thank you,' I said. 'I must go downstairs.' As I began to walk towards the stairs, Mrs Danvers followed me.

'If you want to see the rooms in the west wing, I can show them to you at any time.'

'It's very kind of you, Mrs Danvers,' I said. 'I will let you know.' Mrs Danvers walked beside me.

'Major and Mrs Lacy have been here some time,' she said. 'Didn't you hear their car? Frith took them to the morning-room. I think you know your way now, don't you?'

'Yes, Mrs Danvers,' I said. I knew then that she had been watching me, laughing at my fear. As I went into the drawing-room, I looked back. Mrs Danvers was still watching me from the top of the stairs.

I could hear the sound of voices from the morning-room. I stood for a moment and then walked in.

'Here she is at last,' Maxim said. 'Where have you been hiding? Here is Beatrice and this is Giles. And this is Frank Crawley, our agent[1].'

Beatrice was tall, broad-shouldered and very much like Maxim. She shook hands with me and said to Maxim, 'She's quite different from what I expected. Not like your description at all.'

Everyone laughed, but they seemed friendly. Giles was a big, heavy man. His eyes smiled at me from behind his thick glasses. Frank Crawley was a thin man with a pleasant, worried face. Maxim had told me how hard Frank Crawley worked for Manderley. The men began to talk together and I had to answer Beatrice's questions.

'What do you think of Manderley?' she asked me.

'I haven't seen much of it yet,' I said. 'The house is beautiful, of course. I haven't seen the gardens, but I'm sure I shall never get tired of them. I love walking. I can swim too, when the weather is warmer.'

'My dear, the water is always far too cold here,' said Beatrice.

'I don't mind that, I love swimming. Is it safe to swim in the bays[5]?' Everyone stopped talking. I realized what I had said. Rebecca had been drowned in the bay. I could not look at Maxim. I bent down to stroke the dog's head. Then, thank God, Frith came in to say that lunch was ready. Beatrice walked with me through the hall.

'You know,' she said, 'you are much younger than I expected. Tell me, do you love Maxim very much?'

Beatrice looked at my surprised face and laughed.

'Don't answer,' she said. 'I can see that you do. Maxim looks very well. We were all very worried about him last year. But of course, you know the whole story.'

But Beatrice was wrong. I did not know what had happened

39

down in the bay. Maxim had told me nothing. I had never asked him about Rebecca's death.

Beatrice talked to Maxim all through lunch. Frank Crawley told me a lot about Manderley. I could see that he loved it as much as Maxim did.

When lunch was over, I could see that Maxim was tired. I wished we hadn't had visitors so soon. I took Beatrice out on to the terrace. She asked me how I had met Maxim. I told her about Mrs Van Hopper and how surprised she had been.

'It was rather a shock to us too,' Beatrice said. 'Maxim said in his letter that you were very young and pretty. We expected a very modern sort of girl[2].' Beatrice laughed and I laughed with her.

'Poor Maxim. He had a terrible time,' Beatrice said. 'Let's hope you have made him forget all about it. He loves Manderley so much. But you never know what he is thinking. How do you get on with Mrs Danvers?'

I was surprised by Beatrice's question.

'She frightens me a little,' I said.

'She may try to make things unpleasant for you,' Beatrice went on. 'She's very jealous, of course. She must hate you being here.'

'Why?' I asked. 'Why must she hate me being at Manderley?'

'My dear child,' Beatrice answered slowly, 'I thought Maxim had told you. Mrs Danvers adored Rebecca. She still does.'

At that moment, the men came out of the house. A servant brought rugs[1] and chairs and we all sat under the great tree on the lawn. I hoped everyone would go soon. I wanted to be alone with Maxim. I was sitting on a rug, leaning against Maxim's chair. I listened to the others talking. The afternoon was sleepy and peaceful. Everything was quiet and still. Even the sea seemed far away.

This is what I wanted, I thought. This is how I thought life at Manderley would be.

This moment was safe. It could not be touched. Here we sat

*A servant brought rugs and chairs and we all sat under the
great tree on the lawn.*

together, Maxim and I, hand in hand. The past and the future did not matter at all. At this moment I was not afraid.

The moment passed. Beatrice stood up.

'We must be going,' she said. 'We've got people coming to dinner.' We all got up and Giles looked up at the sky.

'I'm afraid we're going to have some rain,' he said. We all walked slowly back to the drive.

Beatrice took my hand. Then she bent down and kissed me. 'Forgive me if I've asked you a lot of rude questions, my dear. As I said before, you are not what we expected. You are so very different from Rebecca.'

As we reached the car, the sun went behind a cloud and a little rain began to fall. Maxim and I watched the car drive away. We turned and walked back into the house.

8

The Happy Valley

As we stood in the hall, Maxim put his arm round my shoulders.

'Thank God that's over,' he said. 'Get a coat quickly and let's go out. Never mind the rain, I want a walk.'

Maxim looked white and ill. Had Beatrice said something to make him angry? I could not remember.

'Just a moment,' I said. 'I'll get my coat from upstairs.'

'There are plenty of raincoats downstairs,' Maxim said. 'Robert, will you fetch a coat for Mrs de Winter?'

Maxim was standing in the drive now, calling to Jasper.

'Come on, you lazy little fellow. You're too fat.'

Jasper ran round in circles, barking loudly. The young servant, Robert, ran out of the hall, carrying a raincoat. I put it on quickly. It was too big, of course, and too long. But Maxim was waiting impatiently and there was no time to change the coat. We set off together across the lawns to the woods. Jasper ran on in front.

'I soon get tired of my family,' Maxim said. 'Beatrice is very kind-hearted, but she always says the wrong thing.'

I was not sure what Beatrice had said and I thought it better not to ask.

'What did you think of Beatrice?' Maxim asked me. 'What did she talk to you about after lunch?'

'I think I did most of the talking,' I said. 'I was telling her about how we met. She said I was quite different from what she expected.'

'What on earth³ did she expect?'

'Someone much smarter, I think. A modern young woman.'

Maxim did not answer. He bent down and threw a stick for Jasper to run after.

We climbed the grass bank⁶ above the lawns and walked down into the woods. The trees grew very close together over our heads and it was very dark. We walked on last year's leaves. The green shoots of flowers were beginning to show through. Jasper was silent now, with his nose to the ground.

We came to a clearing in the woods. There were two paths, going in opposite directions. Jasper ran on ahead and took the right-hand path without waiting for us.

'Not that way,' called Maxim. 'Come on, old boy.'

The dog looked back at us. He stood there, wagging his tail.

'Why does he want to go that way?' I asked.

'I suppose he's used to it,' Maxim said quickly. 'It leads to a small bay where we used to keep a boat. Come on, Jasper, old boy, this way.'

We turned on to the left-hand path, not saying anything. I looked over my shoulder and saw that Jasper was following us.

'This path brings us to the valley I told you about,' Maxim told me. 'You can smell the flowers already. Never mind the rain, it will bring out the scent.'

Maxim seemed all right again now, happy and cheerful. He began talking about Frank Crawley. He told me what a good agent he was and how he loved Manderley.

I held Maxim's arm and looked up into his face. Talking about Manderley always made Maxim happy again.

We had reached the top of a small hill. The path ran down into a little valley, by the side of a stream.

'There,' said Maxim, 'look at that.'

There were no dark trees in this valley, no thick bushes. On either side of the narrow path stood high graceful bushes covered with flowers. The flowers were pink, white and gold. They were things of beauty and grace. The soft summer rain fell and the air was full of a sweet scent. There was no sound except for the noise of a little stream and the quiet rain on the leaves. When Maxim spoke, his voice was gentle and low.

'We call it the Happy Valley,' he said.

We stood still, not speaking. I looked down at the clear white flowers. Maxim picked up a fallen flower and gave it to me. As I rubbed it between my hands, the scent was sweet and strong.

A bird began to sing, a high, clear sound. Other birds began to sing too. I had never been in so beautiful a place. As we walked along the path, drops of rain fell on my hands and face. I held Maxim's hand. The Happy Valley was the heart of Manderley, the Manderley I would soon know and love.

9

The Cottage in the Bay

We came to the end of the path. The bushes made an arch over our heads so that we had to bend down. I stood straight again, brushing the rain from my head. I saw that the valley was behind us. We were standing in a little narrow bay. There, almost at our feet was the sea.

Maxim looked down at me, smiling at the surprise on my face.

'It is a surprise, isn't it?' he said. 'No one ever expects it.'

Maxim picked up a stone and threw it across the beach[5] for Jasper.

'Fetch it, good boy,' he said. Jasper ran after the stone, barking with excitement.

We both went down to the water's edge and threw more stones. The tide[5] was coming up into the bay and the water was beginning to cover the stones. Maxim turned to me, laughing and wiping the hair out of his eyes. I rolled up the long sleeves of the raincoat. It was a happy moment.

Then we saw that Jasper had gone. We called and whistled, but he did not come.

'Has he gone back to the Happy Valley?' I asked.

'He was by that rock a minute ago,' said Maxim.

We walked up the beach towards the valley again.

'Jasper, Jasper,' called Maxim.

In the distance, beyond a line of rocks to the right of the beach, I heard a sharp bark.

'Do you hear that?' I said. 'He's gone over this way.' I began to climb up the wet rocks.

'Come back,' Maxim said sharply, 'we don't want to go that way.'

'I must get him,' I said. 'He may be hurt.'

'He's all right,' said Maxim. 'Leave him. He knows the way home.'

I began climbing over the rocks towards Jasper. I thought Maxim was being very unkind. I got to the top of the largest rock and looked beyond it. There was another bay. A small stone wall across the bay made it into a small harbour[5]. In the bay was a green and white buoy[5], but no boat.

The woods came right down to the shore. At the edge of the woods was a low stone building, a cottage or a boat-house. There was a man standing on the shore, dressed like a fisherman. Jasper was barking at him and running round and round. The man took no notice of the dog.

'Jasper,' I shouted, 'Jasper, come here.'

The dog looked up, but he did not come to me. I looked back, but I could not see Maxim. I climbed down into the bay and the man looked at me for the first time. There was something strange about him. He had small, stupid looking eyes. His face was fat and round and he had thick, red lips.

'Bad weather, isn't it?' the man said with a stupid smile.

'It's not very nice weather,' I said. 'Come on Jasper, we must go home now.'

But Jasper ran away, barking.

'Have you got any string?' I asked the man. 'I want something to tie the dog. He won't follow me.'

'I know that dog, it's not yours. It comes from the house.'

'He's Mr de Winter's dog,' I said kindly. 'I must take him back.'

The man said nothing, but stared at me in the same stupid way.

I walked up the shore to the cottage. Perhaps there was some string there. The grass round the little house had grown very long. The windows had pieces of wood over them. I pushed at the door. To my surprise it opened and I went inside.

The room was furnished and there were books on the shelves.

*I climbed down into the bay and the man looked at me for the
first time.*

But everything was covered with thick dust. The air was damp and still. Another door at the end of the room led into a small boat-house. I saw some string on a shelf and an old knife. I cut a piece of string for Jasper and went out of the cottage. There was something frightening about that small, dark room. I was glad to be outside again.

The man was still watching me, staring like a child. Jasper was quiet now and let me tie the string.

'I saw you go in there,' the man said. 'She doesn't go in there now. She's gone in the sea. She won't come back, will she?'

'No,' I said. 'She won't come back.'

'I didn't say anything, did I?' The man's eyes were full of fear. He turned away and walked back towards the sea.

Maxim was waiting for me beside the rocks. He looked angry.

'I'm sorry,' I said. 'I had to get some string for Jasper. Who is that man?'

'That's Ben. He's a bit mad, but he won't hurt you. Where did you get that string?'

'I found it in the cottage. The door was open. There's dust everywhere. The place ought to be cleaned.'

'The door should be locked,' Maxim said. He was walking very fast now. He went up past the cottage and on to a path through the woods. It was very different here from the Happy Valley. The path was steep and the trees were thick, and dark. It was cold now and my legs ached[6]. Jasper was tired too, and walked very slowly.

'Come on, Jasper, for God's sake[3],' said Maxim angrily. 'Pull at that string, can't you?' he said to me.

'It's your fault,' I said, 'you walk so fast.'

'If you had listened to me, we would be home by now. There was no need for you to go after Jasper.'

'I thought you would come with me,' I answered.

'Why should I run after the damned[3] dog?' Maxim said, not looking at me.

'That's an excuse. You didn't want to go over the rocks,' I answered.

'All right, I didn't. I didn't want to go to the other bay. I never go near the place or that damned cottage. If you had my memories, you would not go there either. You wouldn't talk about it or even think about it.'

Maxim's face was white. His eyes had a dark, lost look. I took his hand and held it tight.

'Please, Maxim, please,' I said. 'I don't want you to look like that. I'm sorry, darling. Please don't let us quarrel.'

'We should have stayed in Italy,' Maxim said. 'I was a fool to bring you back to Manderley.'

I had to run to keep up with him now. At last we came to the top of the path and out on to the lawn. Maxim's face was hard. He walked straight into the house and spoke to Frith.

'We want tea at once,' said Maxim. Then he went quickly into the library and shut the door.

I tried to keep back my tears. Frith must not see them. I turned away as he helped me off with the raincoat. He picked up a handkerchief.

'Is this yours, Madam?' he said.

I put the handkerchief in my pocket and walked slowly across the hall to the library. Maxim was sitting in his usual chair, with Jasper at his feet. I walked across the room and knelt down by Maxim's chair.

'Don't be angry with me any more,' I said.

Maxim looked down at me.

'I'm not angry with you,' he said.

'But I've made you unhappy,' I replied. 'I want you to be happy so much. I love you.'

'Do you?' he said. His eyes were full of pain and fear.

'What is it, darling?' I said. 'Why do you look like that?'

The door opened before Maxim could answer. It was Frith and Robert with the tea. The small table was put near the fire and covered with the white cloth. Frith brought in the silver teapot and kettle. Then came the cups, the sandwiches and cakes. Everything was the same as yesterday. When the servants had gone, I looked at Maxim's face. The colour had come back into it. He took a sandwich.

'Pour me a cup of tea, darling,' he said to me. 'And forgive me for being so unkind.'

There was nothing more to say. Maxim smiled at me and picked up his paper. Maxim's smile was like a pat[6] on the head given to Jasper.

I was not hungry and I felt very tired. I gave Jasper a piece of cake and took out the handkerchief to wipe my hands. The handkerchief was not mine. It must have come from the raincoat pocket. There were some letters in the corner – a tall "R" and "de W." It was Rebecca's. The raincoat, too wide, too long for me, must have been hers too. Rebecca had worn that raincoat. She had left the handkerchief in the pocket. I could smell a scent, a scent I knew. I shut my eyes and tried to remember what it was.

Suddenly I knew. The scent on the handkerchief was the scent of the flowers in the Happy Valley. Was there nowhere I could escape from Rebecca?

10

Questions and Answers

The weather was wet and cold for over a week. We did not go down to the beach again. I could see the sea from the terrace[1] and the lawns. It looked cold and grey. When I stood on the terrace, I could hear the sound of great waves on the shore. I began to understand why some people hated the low, angry voice of the sea. I was glad that our rooms were in the east wing. If I could not sleep, I went to the window and looked out on to the rose-garden. I was not troubled by the sea's unhappy music.

Sometimes I thought about the cottage down in the bay. There were so many questions I wanted to ask Maxim. I could not forget the lost look in Maxim's eyes. I could not forget his words: 'I was a fool to bring you back to Manderley.'

It was all my fault. I had gone down into the bay. I had reminded Maxim of the past. We lived our lives together sleeping, eating, walking. But, every hour of the day, the past made a wall between us.

I became nervous and afraid. I did not want anyone to talk about the sea or boats. When visitors came to Manderley, I was shy and awkward. I knew that they compared me with Rebecca. She had been charming, interested in everyone. I was dull and stupid, like a schoolgirl.

One afternoon, I was having tea alone when the wife of the bishop[6] called. She was a kind woman and tried hard to make me talk. At last she said,

'Will your husband hold the Manderley Fancy Dress Ball[1] this year? I remember the last one so well. It was such a lovely sight. I shall never forget it.'

I smiled and said, 'We have not decided. There have been so many things to do.'

I could not tell the woman that Maxim had never spoken about the ball.

'Manderley looked so beautiful,' the bishop's wife went on. 'And there was dancing, and music and flowers everywhere.'

'Yes,' I said. 'Yes, I must ask Maxim about it.'

'We came to a garden-party too, one summer,' the bishop's wife went on. 'It was a lovely day. We all had tea in the rose-garden. It was such a clever idea. Of course, she was a clever person.'

She stopped, her face rather red. I heard myself saying, 'Rebecca must have been a wonderful person. . .'

I had said her name at last. 'Rebecca.' I had said it aloud.

'You never met her then?' the woman asked. 'Yes, she was a lovely person. So full of life. Everyone loved her.'

'She was so good at everything too,' I said. 'Clever, beautiful and fond of sport.'

'Rebecca was certainly beautiful,' my visitor went on. 'I remember her on the night of the Ball. She had a cloud[6] of dark hair. Her skin was very white. And she had such a lovely dress.'

'She looked after everything in the house, too,' I said. 'I'm afraid I leave it all to the housekeeper.'

'Oh well, you are very young, aren't you? We can't all do everything. I must go now. Do ask your husband to have another ball.'

'Yes, of course I will.'

I sat in the library after my visitor had gone. I thought about Manderley, full of people in beautiful costumes, dancing in the hall. I thought of Rebecca, lively and beautiful, arranging everything. What must people think about me?

I suddenly sat up straight. I did not mind. I did not care. I was Mrs de Winter now, not Rebecca. I decided that I would find out more about the Fancy Dress Ball. But I did not want to ask Maxim.

Later that afternoon, Frank Crawley came up to the house.

'I have been hearing about the Fancy Dress Ball, Frank,' I said. 'I did not know you had dances here.'

Frank did not reply at once. Then he said, 'The Manderley Ball was held every year. People came from miles around. They even came down from London.'

'It must have been a lot of work,' I said. 'I suppose Rebecca did most of it.'

Frank looked straight ahead.

'We all helped,' he said.

'Will you ask Maxim about the Ball?' I asked. 'It does seem a good idea.'

Frank did not answer me.

'I went into that cottage in the bay a few days ago,' I said. 'It's very dirty. Why doesn't someone do something about it?'

'Maxim would tell me if he wanted anything done,' Frank replied.

'Are they Rebecca's things?' I asked.

'Yes,' Frank said.

'Did Rebecca use the cottage a lot?'

'Yes, she did. She slept in the cottage sometimes. She had moonlight picnics[1] on the shore.'

I noticed that Frank always called Rebecca 'she'. He never used her name.

'Why is there a buoy in the bay?' I asked. 'There's no boat there. What happened to it? Was it the boat Rebecca was sailing when she died?'

'Yes,' said Frank, quietly. 'It turned over and sank. She was washed overboard and drowned. The sea is sometimes very rough in the bay.'

'Couldn't anyone have helped her?' I asked.

'Nobody saw the accident. Nobody knew she was sailing. She often went out alone like that.'

'When did they find her?' I felt I must know everything now. I had been thinking about that terrible night for so long.

'They found her two months later. The sea had carried her forty miles up the coast. Maxim had to identify the body[4].'

Suddenly I was ashamed of all my questions.

'Frank,' I said, 'I'm sorry I asked you all those questions. But everything is so strange to me at Manderley. And when I meet anyone new, I know what they are thinking: "How different she is from Rebecca." '

'Mrs de Winter, you mustn't think that,' said Frank, looking at me for the first time. 'I am so glad you have married Maxim. It will make such a difference to his life. And Manderley needs someone like you, someone young, fresh and charming.'

'But Rebecca was so charming – and clever. People still remember her.'

'Maxim would be very unhappy to hear you talking like this, Mrs de Winter. Forget the past, as Maxim has done. None of us want to bring back the past. Your job here is to lead us away from it.'

I was much happier now. But I had to ask Frank one more question.

'Tell me, Frank,' I said. 'Was Rebecca very beautiful?'

Frank turned away from me so that I could not see his face.

'Yes,' he said slowly. 'Yes, I suppose she was the most beautiful woman I ever saw in my life.'

11

The China Cupid[1]

I did not see very much of Mrs Danvers. She sent the menus to the morning-room every day. She rang me every morning on the house telephone. She had also found a maid for me, called Clarice. Clarice was new to Manderley and this was her first job. Her family lived near Manderley, but she had never known Rebecca. To Clarice, I was an important person because I was Mrs de Winter.

Mrs Danvers was certainly an excellent housekeeper and I began to lose my fear of her. Sometimes I felt sorry for Mrs Danvers. It must hurt her to call me Mrs de Winter when, all the time, she was thinking about Rebecca.

Frank had told me to forget the past. I wanted to. But Frank did not sit in the morning-room every day as I did. He did not sit at Rebecca's desk and touch the things she had touched. Dear God[3], I did not want to think about Rebecca. I wanted to be happy. I wanted Maxim to be happy too. But Rebecca was always in my thoughts and dreams.

Beatrice, Maxim's sister, had promised to give me a wedding present. She did not forget. One day, Robert brought a large parcel into the morning-room where I was sitting alone. I cut the string excitedly and tore off the dark brown paper. Beatrice had sent me four big books about painting. She knew that I enjoyed sketching and she had really tried to please me.

I was glad to have something at Manderley that belonged to me. I looked round the room for somewhere to put the books. I stood them in a row on top of the desk and looked at them. But the books were far too heavy. First one fell and then the others followed. A little china ornament which always stood on the desk was knocked on to the floor. The ornament broke into many pieces. It was a beautiful little cupid and one of the loveliest things in the house. I was suddenly very frightened. I found an envelope in a drawer and carefully put the pieces of china into it. Then, like a child, I hid the envelope in the desk. I decided to put my new books in the library and I said nothing about the cupid.

The following day, after lunch, Frith brought our coffee to the library as usual. Instead of leaving, he stood by Maxim's chair.

'Could I speak to you, sir?' he said. Maxim looked up from his paper.

'Yes, Frith, what is it?'

'It's about Robert, sir. He's very upset. Mrs Danvers has accused him of taking a valuable ornament from the morning-room. Mrs Danvers noticed it was missing late this morning. She

I found an envelope in a drawer and carefully put the pieces of china into it.

says that Robert must have taken it or broken it. Robert says he knows nothing about it.'

'Perhaps it was one of the maids,' said Maxim. I knew he hated any kind of trouble with the servants.

'No, sir. No one except Robert has been in the room, apart from Madam, of course. Mrs Danvers doesn't let the maids clean the morning-room.'

'Well, Mrs Danvers had better come and see me. What ornament was it?'

'The china cupid, sir. It stands on the desk.'

'Oh dear,' said Maxim. 'That's very valuable. It must be found. I'll see Mrs Danvers at once.'

'Very good, sir,' said Frith and quietly left the room.

'Darling,' I said to Maxim when we were alone, 'I meant to tell you before, but I forgot. I broke the cupid yesterday.'

'You broke it? Why didn't you say so when Frith was here? You'll have to explain to Mrs Danvers now.'

'Oh no. Please, Maxim, you tell her. Let me go upstairs.'

'Don't be silly,' said Maxim angrily. 'Anyone would think you were afraid of Mrs Danvers.'

'I am afraid of her. At least not afraid, but. . .'

The door opened without a sound and Mrs Danvers came into the room. I looked nervously at Maxim. His face was half amused, half angry.

'It's all a mistake, Mrs Danvers,' Maxim told her. 'Mrs de Winter broke the cupid herself. She forgot to tell us.'

I felt like a child again.

'I'm so sorry,' I said, 'I never thought Robert would get into trouble.'

'Is it possible to repair the cupid, Madam?' said Mrs Danvers. She did not seem surprised. I felt she had known the truth all the time.

'I'm afraid not,' I said. 'It's in hundreds of pieces.'

'What did you do with the pieces?' said Maxim.

57

'They are in an envelope in a drawer of the writing desk.'

'Find the pieces, Mrs Danvers. Try to get them mended in London.'

'I never thought that Mrs de Winter had broken the ornament,' said Mrs Danvers. As she left the room I could see the scorn and hatred in her eyes.

'I'm very sorry, darling,' I said. 'It was very silly and careless of me.'

'Forget it,' said Maxim. 'But you do act strangely sometimes. More like a servant than the mistress of Manderley. Even when we have visitors, you sit on the edge of your chair and say only "yes" and "no".'

'I can't help being shy.'

'I know you can't, darling. But you must learn to hide it.'

'I do try. But I'm not used to this kind of life. People look at me and ask me so many questions.'

'What does it matter? They are interested in us, that's all.'

'They can't find me very interesting,' I said. 'I suppose that's why you married me. You knew I was dull and quiet. No one would ever gossip about me.'

Maxim threw his paper on the ground and got up from his chair. His face was dark with anger and his voice was hard.

'What do you know about any gossip down here?' he said. 'Who's been talking to you?'

'No one. No one at all.'

Maxim stared at me.

'Perhaps I did a very selfish thing when I married you,' he said slowly. 'I am so much older than you.'

I felt cold and frightened.

'Age doesn't matter,' I said. 'I'm happy. You know I love you more than anything else in the world. I love Manderley too. I love everything here. You're happy too, darling, aren't you?'

Maxim did not answer. He stood staring out of the window.

'If you don't think we're happy, you must tell me,' I went on. 'I don't want you to lie to me.'

Maxim took my face in his hands.

'How can I answer you?' he said. 'If you are happy, then we are both happy.'

He kissed me and walked across the room.

'But you are disappointed in me. You think I am not right for Manderley. If only I hadn't broken that cupid. Was it very valuable?'

'I think so,' Maxim answered. 'It was a wedding present. Rebecca knew a lot about china.'

Maxim went on staring straight in front of him.

He is thinking about Rebecca, I said to myself. I have broken one of their wedding presents.

Maxim went back to his chair and picked up his paper. I sat on the long seat under the window. After a time, Jasper came to me and climbed on to my lap.

12

In the West Wing

Maxim had to go up to London at the end of June. It was the first time that I had been left alone at Manderley. I was sure that Maxim would have a terrible accident or even be killed. I was too worried to eat any lunch. At about two o'clock, Robert brought me a message. Maxim had arrived safely in London after a good journey. I felt happy again and also rather hungry. I went back into the dining-room and took an apple and some biscuits. Then I called Jasper and we went together into the woods.

As I sat there I felt happier than I had ever been at Manderley. I could not understand it. I had not wanted Maxim to go to London, but now I was glad to be alone.

I walked through the Happy Valley to the bay. The sea was very calm. Jasper ran up the rocks leading to the next bay.

'Not that way, Jasper,' I called. The dog took no notice.

Oh well, it doesn't matter, I thought. Maxim isn't here. And I climbed over the rocks after Jasper.

The tide was out and there was very little water in the bay. The white and green buoy was still there. I could read the name on it now: *Je Reviens*. A strange name for a boat – "I'll come back". And that boat would never come back now.

I walked slowly across the beach to the cottage. The sun was shining today and the cottage did not look frightening any more. I pushed open the door. Everything was exactly as before. There was a sound in the boat-house and Jasper ran up to the doorway, barking angrily.

'Is anybody there?' I said.

I looked through the door and saw Ben sitting by the wall. He looked very frightened.

'I think you should come out,' I said. 'Mr de Winter doesn't like people coming in here.'

Ben followed me out into the sunshine.

'I'm not doing anything wrong,' he said. 'You won't lock me up, will you?'

His whole body was shaking with fear and tears were rolling down his fat, round face.

'I didn't do anything. I didn't tell anyone,' he said.

'That's all right, Ben. No one's going to hurt you. But don't go into the cottage again.'

Ben smiled.

'You're not like the other one,' he said. 'She was tall and dark. She had eyes like a snake. She came here at night. She saw me once, looking at her. "You'll be locked up. People will hurt you," she said. But you won't lock me up, will you?'

'No, of course not, Ben,' I said.

Ben smiled again and went off down the beach to the sea. I went up towards the wood. Jasper followed me. When I looked back, Ben had gone. But I had a strange feeling that someone was watching me. Someone tall and dark, who watched and listened.

––––––

I started to run up the path and did not feel safe until I reached the lawn. The house stood there, safe and secure. The sun shone on something metal in the drive. A green sports car was parked there. I had never seen it before and I hoped the visitor did not want to stay to tea.

As I walked across the lawn, I looked up at the west wing. One of the shutters[1] was open and a man stood at the window. Then another figure, dressed in black, closed the shutter. I was sure it was Mrs Danvers. But who was the man? And why had he come when Maxim was away in London?

I walked up the steps, through the hall and into the morning-room. I could smell cigarette smoke. Then I heard voices and, without thinking, I hid behind the door. I heard Mrs Danvers say, 'I expect she went into the library. Wait here while I go and see.'

She was talking about me of course. I did not know what to do. Jasper had moved towards the drawing-room, wagging his tail.

'Hallo, Jasper, old boy,' said a man's voice and Jasper ran back into the morning-room. The man followed. He saw me standing behind the door. I have never seen anyone more surprised.

'I beg your pardon,' the man said, looking down at me with a rather unpleasant smile. He was a big, handsome man, but his face was red and his eyes were a hard blue. His breath smelt of whisky.

'I'm so sorry,' he said. 'I called to see Danny. She's an old friend of mine.'

He lit a cigarette and looked round the room.

'How's old Max?' he asked.

'Maxim's very well. He's in London,' I said.

'What? He's left you all alone? That's not fair, is it?' The man gave an unpleasant laugh. I did not like him at all.

At that moment, Mrs Danvers came back. She looked at me angrily.

'Well, Danny,' the man said, 'aren't you going to introduce me to the new bride?'

'This is Mr Favell, Madam,' said Mrs Danvers.

'How do you do?' I said politely. 'Will you stay to tea?'

The man laughed again.

'Now isn't that kind, Danny,' he said. 'But I had better be going. Come and look at my car,' he said to me. 'It's a good car. Much faster than the one Max has.'

I did not like the way that Favell spoke about Maxim. I did not want to look at his car. But I followed him out into the hall.

'Goodbye, Danny. Take care of yourself. You know my telephone number.'

'Dear old Manderley,' Favell said as we walked out of the house. 'What do you think of it? Aren't you lonely living here?'

'I'm very fond of Manderley,' I said.

'I have enjoyed meeting you,' Favell said, standing by his car. 'But I'd rather you didn't tell Max about my visit. I'm afraid your husband doesn't like me very much. He might be cross[2] with poor old Danny.'

'No, all right,' I said awkwardly. 'I won't say anything to Maxim.'

He got into the car and started the engine.

'That's very kind,' he said. 'Perhaps I'll come back and see you one day. Goodbye.'

Favell drove away noisily and much too fast. I walked slowly back to the house. Mrs Danvers had gone. I wondered who Favell was. He had certainly been to Manderley before. And, like

'This is Mr Favell, Madam,' said Mrs Danvers.

Rebecca, he called Maxim 'Max'. Had Favell known Rebecca? What had he been doing in the west wing? There were some very valuable things in the house. Perhaps the man was a thief.

I decided to go up to the west wing. I must see that everything was all right. The house seemed very quiet as I began to walk up the stairs. My heart was beating in a strange, excited way.

I was again in the corridor where I had stood on my first morning at Manderley. I turned the handle of the nearest door and went inside. Everything was dark. I found the light and switched it on. I was surprised to see that the room was completely furnished. There was no dust and everything was clean and tidy. The room, a bedroom, was the most beautiful I had ever seen. There were flowers on the dressing table and on the table beside the bed. A satin dressing-gown lay on a chair. There was a pair of slippers under a chair.

I walked slowly into the middle of the room. No, it was not used. It was not lived in any more. The air was not fresh. Rebecca would never come back to this room again. I could hear the sea clearly. I went to the window and opened a shutter. Yes, I was standing at the window where I had seen Mrs Danvers and Favell.

I felt afraid and my legs began to tremble. I sat down on the stool by the dressing-table. I looked round the room, the most beautiful in Manderley. A room that was never used now.

I got up and went to the chair. I touched the satin dressing-gown. I picked up the slippers and held them in my hand.

On the bed lay Rebecca's nightdress. I went to the bed and held the nightdress to my face. It was cold and smelt of the flowers in the Happy Valley.

As I stood looking down at the bed, I heard a step behind me. I turned quickly. It was Mrs Danvers. I shall never forget the look

I shall never forget the look on Mrs Danvers' face. It was a look of strange, terrible excitement.

on her face. It was a look of strange, terrible excitement.

She came nearer and I could feel her breath on my face.

'Is there anything the matter, Madam? Are you feeling unwell?' Mrs Danvers said quietly.

'I did not expect to see you here, Mrs Danvers. I came up to fasten one of the shutters.'

'I will fasten it,' Mrs Danvers said.

Mrs Danvers came back from the window and stood beside me.

'You opened the shutter yourself, didn't you?' she said. 'You wanted to see this room, didn't you? Now you are here, let me show you everything.'

Her voice now was as soft and sweet as honey.

'It's a lovely room, isn't it? That was her bed. I keep it just as it was. This was her nightdress. She was wearing it the night before she died. These are her slippers.'

Mrs Danvers put the slippers back under the chair and walked across the room to a large wardrobe.

'All her evening clothes are here. Her furs, too. Mr de Winter was always buying clothes for her, beautiful clothes.'

Mrs Danvers held my arm tightly with her long thin fingers. Her eyes looked deep into mine.

'I blame myself for the accident,' she said. 'I was out that evening. When I came in, I heard she had gone down to the bay. I was worried. The wind was blowing hard. Mr de Winter came in at about eleven. The wind was blowing harder, and still she had not come back.

'I sat on my bed until after five. Then I put on my coat and went down to the bay. I saw at once that the boat had gone.'

Mrs Danvers' hand fell back to her side.

'That is why Mr de Winter doesn't use these rooms any more. Listen to the sea.'

Even with the shutters and windows closed, I could hear the dull, harsh sound of the sea in the bay.

'I come into these rooms and dust them every day,' Mrs Danvers said. 'If you want to come again, ask me. No one comes here but me.

'Sometimes I feel she is standing here, behind me. I feel her everywhere. In the morning-room and in the hall. You feel her too, don't you?'

I tried to smile, but I felt sick and ill.

'Do you think she can see us now?' Mrs Danvers asked me. 'Do you think the dead watch the living?'

'I don't know,' I said. 'I don't know.'

'Sometimes I think she watches you and Mr de Winter together,' Mrs Danvers whispered.

We stood there by the door, staring at one another. I could not take my eyes away from hers. Then I turned and walked into the corridor. I went down the stairs and through the door to the east wing. I pushed open the door to my own bedroom. I shut the door of the room and locked it.

Then I lay down on my bed and closed my eyes. I felt terribly sick.

13

More About Jack Favell

Maxim rang up the next morning. I heard the phone ring while I was having breakfast and Frith answered it. I hoped that Maxim would ask for me but he did not.

'Mr de Winter will be back at about six this evening,' Frith told me.

'All right, Frith. Thank you,' I said.

I went on eating breakfast as slowly as I could. Jasper was sitting at my feet. I wondered what I should do all day. I had slept badly. I could not forget my visit to the west wing. I knew now how much Mrs Danvers hated me.

About ten o'clock, the telephone rang again. This time it was Beatrice.

'Well, my dear, how are you?' she said. 'Shall I come and have lunch with you today?'

'I'd like you to come very much, Beatrice,' I said.

'All right, my dear. See you later.'

I put the phone down. I was glad that Beatrice was coming. It gave me something to look forward to. I wandered out on to the lawn. I felt different from yesterday. I wanted Maxim to come home.

I tried not to remember my visit to the west wing. But I could not stop thinking about Favell and his friendship with Mrs Danvers. I began to feel that Mrs Danvers was watching me. There were so many rooms that Maxim and I never used. It was easy for Mrs Danvers to watch me from one of their windows.

Beatrice arrived by car at about half past twelve. This time I went out to the drive to meet her.

'Well, my dear, here I am,' she said. 'It's a lovely day, isn't it?'

She gave me a kiss and then looked at me carefully.

'You don't look well,' Beatrice said. 'You are much too thin. Your face is pale, too. What's wrong with you?'

'Nothing,' I said. 'My face is always pale.'

'You looked quite different when I saw you before,' Beatrice told me. 'You are not going to have a baby, are you?'

'No, I don't think so,' I said.

'Well, I hope you will sometime. Maxim would be so happy to have a son. What have you been doing with yourself? Have you done much sketching? Did you like the books I sent you? Have you had anyone to stay?'

I had forgotten that Beatrice asked so many questions.

'No, we've had no one to stay. People come to tea sometimes, of course.'

I wondered whether to tell Beatrice about Mrs Danvers' visitor, Favell. I did not want Beatrice to tell Maxim about the visit. But I did want to find out more about the man.

'Have you ever heard of a man called Jack Favell, Beatrice?' I asked her.

'Jack Favell?' said Beatrice slowly. 'Yes, I do know the name. Wait a minute – Jack Favell. Yes, of course. I remember him now. He's an awful[2] man. I met him once, years ago.'

'He was here yesterday,' I told her. 'He came to see Mrs Danvers.'

Beatrice did not look at me.

'Oh well,' she said, 'I suppose he knows Mrs Danvers quite well.'

'But why?' I asked.

'Jack Favell is Rebecca's cousin,' Beatrice said. 'I think he came to Manderley quite a lot when Rebecca was alive. I'm not sure.'

'I did not like him,' I said.

'No, I don't suppose that you did,' Beatrice answered.

I hoped that she would tell me more about Favell, but she did not. For the rest of the time we talked about other things.

Beatrice stayed for tea and left soon afterwards. She had promised to meet her husband, Giles, at the station.

'I hope you won't be so thin next time I see you,' Beatrice said as she got into her car. 'Give Maxim my love. Look after him, and look after yourself, too.'

I watched Beatrice's car go down the drive. Maxim would not be back for another hour. I did not feel like sitting in the house by myself. I called Jasper and we went for a walk through the woods. But I did not go near the sea. I missed[2] Maxim now and felt lonely without him. Beatrice's questions had made me feel tired too.

When I came back from my walk, I saw Maxim's car standing in front of the house. At once, I felt much happier. I ran quickly up the steps and into the hall. As I walked towards the library, I heard the sound of voices. One voice was Maxim's, very loud and angry. The door was shut, but I could hear what he said.

'You can tell Favell to keep away from Manderley. Tell him I said so,' Maxim was saying.

'I know he was here. Never mind who told me. His car was seen here yesterday. If you want to meet him, meet him somewhere else. I don't want that man at Manderley. I won't even have him in the gardens. I'm telling you for the last time.'

I heard footsteps. I ran quickly up the stairs and hid myself.

Mrs Danvers came out of the library. She shut the door and walked up the stairs. Her face was grey with anger and the look in her eyes frightened me. Thank God she did not know I was watching her. Mrs Danvers went through the door to the west wing.

I waited a moment and then went downstairs and into the library. Maxim was standing by the window. When he heard the door open, he turned round quickly.

I smiled and held out my hand to him.

'Oh, it's you,' Maxim said.

I could tell that he was very angry. His face was white and his mouth hard. I took his hand in mine.

'I missed you so much,' I said. 'I hate being here without you.'

'Do you?' Maxim said. He did not say anything about Mrs Danvers or Favell.

'Are you worried about something?' I asked.

'I've had a long day,' Maxim answered. 'And London was very hot and noisy. I always hate going there.'

Maxim lit a cigarette and moved away from me. I knew then that he was not going to tell me about his anger with Mrs Danvers. Maxim still thought of me as a child – someone who must not hear unpleasant things. But he was wrong. I felt I was growing up a little more every day. My life at Manderley was turning me into a woman.

14

Preparations for the Ball

It was on a Sunday afternoon when someone spoke about the Fancy Dress Ball again. Frank Crawley had come to lunch and the three of us were hoping to have a quiet afternoon. But as we were walking out to the big tree on the lawn, we heard a car in the drive. We had to go back into the house to welcome the visitors. Very soon, more people arrived and then some more.

They all stayed to tea, of course. As we sat in the drawing-room eating cake and sandwiches, one of our visitors suddenly said to Maxim, 'Oh, Mr de Winter. There is something I must ask you. Are you having a Fancy Dress Ball at Manderley this year?'

Maxim answered quietly.

'I haven't thought about it,' he said. 'And I don't think anyone else has, either.'

'Oh, but you are wrong,' said another woman. 'We have all been thinking about it. We used to enjoy the Manderley Ball so much.'

'Well, I don't know,' said Maxim. 'There would be a great deal to do. You had better ask Frank Crawley. He would do most of the work.'

'I don't mind the work,' said Frank, looking at me. 'It's for Maxim and Mrs de Winter to decide.'

Everyone looked at me and started to talk at once.

'Now, Mrs de Winter, you must help us. Your husband will listen to you. After all, you are a new bride. The Ball will be for you.'

'Yes, of course,' said a man, 'we all missed² your wedding. There ought to be some kind of party here at Manderley.'

Everyone laughed and clapped their hands.

Maxim looked at me.

'What about you? Would you like it?' he said.

I did not know what Maxim was thinking. Perhaps he thought I was too shy to want the Ball.

'I think I rather like the idea,' I said with a smile.

Maxim turned away.

'All right, then, Frank. We'll have the dance. Mrs Danvers can help you. She will know what to do. Now, if we've all finished tea, we'll go into the garden.'

We all went outside. Our visitors were talking happily now about their costumes[6] for the Ball. I felt excited too.

'What will you wear?' I said to Maxim.

'I never wear fancy dress,' Maxim replied. 'I'm the host, so I can do as I like.'

'What shall I wear?' I said. 'I've no idea at all.'

Maxim smiled at me.

'If you look pretty, I don't mind what you put on,' he told me.

'All right,' I said. 'My costume will be a secret. I shall keep it as a surprise.'

Maxim laughed and patted me on the shoulder. As usual, he was treating me like a child. I did not want to be a child. I wanted to be a grown-up woman.

I shall wear a beautiful dress at the Ball, I told myself. Everyone will say how charming I am. They will think of me as the real Mrs de Winter at last. Maxim will love me as his wife and forget about Rebecca.

Soon everyone at Manderley was talking about the Fancy Dress Ball. My little maid, Clarice, spoke of nothing else.

'Oh, Madam, it's so exciting,' she said. 'I'm looking forward[2] to it so much.'

The preparations went on. Frank was very busy and so was Mrs Danvers. I saw very little of her, and I was glad.

I began to get worried about my costume. I did not know what to wear. I looked through the books that Beatrice had given me. I made sketches of some of the costumes, but I did not like any of them. I wanted something that was pretty and simple too.

That evening, as I was getting ready for dinner, there was a knock at my bedroom door. To my surprise, it was Mrs Danvers. She was holding a piece of paper in her hand. It was a drawing of a costume which I had sketched and then thrown away.

'I found this, Madam,' Mrs Danvers said. 'I thought you had thrown it away by mistake.'

'No, Mrs Danvers, I don't want it, thank you,' I said quickly.

I hoped she would go, but she stood at the door.

'So you haven't decided what to wear, Madam,' Mrs Danvers said in a friendly voice.

'No, I haven't decided yet,' I replied.

'Perhaps you could copy[6] one of the pictures in the gallery,' Mrs Danvers suggested. 'Many of them would make beautiful costumes. What does Mr de Winter think?'

'I don't know,' I said. 'I wanted to surprise him. I was going to keep my costume a secret.'

Mrs Danvers looked pleased at my words.

'Then I suggest that you have your costume made in London, Madam. There is a shop in Bond Street[6] that would do it really well. I have always liked the picture of the girl in white,' Mrs Danvers went on in the same friendly way.

'The picture is about two hundred years old. The girl's wearing a very simple dress. It would be easy to copy.'

I did not know what to say. I knew the picture well. I wished I had thought of the idea myself.

'Thank you, Mrs Danvers,' I said.

Mrs Danvers went out quietly. I wondered why she was so friendly. Perhaps Maxim's anger had frightened her a little.

As I went down to dinner, I stopped in front of the picture of the young girl. Her name was Caroline de Winter and she had been famous for her beauty. The dress was very simple, with short

I stopped in front of the picture of Caroline de Winter.

sleeves and a long, full skirt. Her hair was in curls. I would have to wear a wig[6] over my own straight hair. I felt very excited. I was glad that I had chosen my costume at last. I said nothing to Maxim. The next day I made a sketch of the picture. Then I sent the drawing to the shop in London with careful instructions about the dress and the wig.

The preparations for the great day went on. No one expected me to do anything. Slowly, the great house began to change. Furniture was moved as the great hall was prepared for dancing. Coloured lights were hung in the trees outside. There were flowers everywhere. Hundreds of them were brought in from the garden and Mrs Danvers knew exactly how to arrange them. Manderley took on a new beauty. I had never seen the old house looking so lovely.

15

'Miss Caroline de Winter'

On the day of the Ball, Maxim and I had lunch with Frank. My dress and the wig had arrived and they both looked perfect. Maxim and Frank asked me about my costume but I told them nothing. The secret made me feel excited and important.

'You won't know it's me,' I told them. 'You will both have the surprise of your lives.'

Maxim and I went back to the house after lunch. The band had arrived and we welcomed the men. The afternoon seemed very long. I thought about going for a walk. Then suddenly, it was tea-time and Beatrice and her husband, Giles, had arrived.

'This is like old times,' said Beatrice, looking around. 'Everything is as beautiful as ever. What's everyone going to wear? I suppose you refuse to wear fancy dress, Maxim?'

'Of course,' Maxim said. 'I prefer to be comfortable.'

'I'm going to dress as an Arab,' said Giles. 'I got the idea from a friend.'

'What about you, Mrs Lacy?' Frank said to Beatrice.

'I'm in Eastern dress, too. I'm wearing a veil and lots of jewellery. I'll be cool and comfortable. That's all that matters.'

Beatrice turned to me.

'And what is our hostess[1] going to wear?' she asked. 'The Ball is for you, after all. We all expect you to wear something really special.'

'Don't ask her,' said Maxim. 'She won't tell anyone. She's had the dress made in London.'

'It's quite simple really,' I said.

'What fun it all is,' said Beatrice. 'I'm getting excited already.'

'You've got her to thank for it,' said Maxim, smiling at me.

Everyone looked at me and smiled. I felt pleased and happy. This Ball was for me because I was a bride, the new Mrs de Winter. Manderley had been made into a place of light and beauty, just for me.

'What's the time?' I said. 'I think we ought to be getting ready.'

I found Clarice waiting for me in my bedroom, her face full of excitement. I locked the door and took the dress from its box. It fitted perfectly. I looked at myself in the mirror. I smiled. I felt different already. I was someone more exciting and interesting than my usual self.

'Give me the wig, Clarice,' I said. 'Be careful, the curls mustn't be flat.'

I brushed back my own straight hair. Carefully, I put the wig in place. I looked in the mirror again. The wig and the tightly fitting[6] dress made me almost beautiful.

'Oh, Clarice,' I said. 'What will Mr de Winter say?'

There was a knock on the door.

'Who's there?' I called. 'You can't come in.'

'It's me, my dear,' said Beatrice. 'Are you ready? I want to have a look at you.'

'No, no,' I said, 'you can't come in. Tell Maxim that he can't come in either. I'll come down when I'm ready.'

I looked in the mirror again. My eyes looked larger and the curls made a soft cloud round my head. I lifted the skirt of the dress in my hands.

'Unlock the door,' I said to Clarice. 'I'm going down.'

I stood in the gallery and looked down on the hall below.

There was Giles in his white Arab costume. Beatrice was wearing a long green dress. Frank was dressed as a sailor. Only Maxim was wearing evening clothes.

'I don't know what she's doing,' I heard Maxim say. 'What's the time, Frank? She must be down soon.'

I looked up at the picture of Caroline de Winter. Yes, her dress was exactly like mine and she had the same curled hair. The band was playing softly in the gallery.

'Beat the drum,' I said, 'and call out: Miss Caroline de Winter.'

The drum sounded. Everyone looked up.

'Miss Caroline de Winter,' the man shouted.

I stood at the top of the stairs, smiling. I expected everyone to laugh and clap as I walked down the stairs.

Nobody laughed. Nobody clapped. They all stared at me without moving. I smiled at Maxim.

'How do you do, Mr de Winter?' I said.

Maxim stared up at me. His face was completely white. Something was wrong. Why was Maxim looking like that? He moved towards the stairs.

'What the hell[3] do you think you're doing?' he said.

His eyes were on fire with anger.

'It's the picture,' I said. 'The one in the gallery.'

There was a long silence. Still nobody moved.

'What is it?' I said. 'What have I done?'

77

I stood at the top of the stairs, smiling.

When Maxim answered, his voice was cold and hard.

'Go and take off that dress. It doesn't matter what you wear. Any evening dress will do. Go quickly, before anyone comes.'

I could not speak. I stood staring at Maxim.

'What are you standing there for?' he asked me. 'Didn't you hear what I said?'

I turned and ran up the stairs. My eyes were full of tears. I did not know what I was doing. The door to the west wing was open. Mrs Danvers was standing there. I shall never forget the terrible look on her face. It was a look of joy – of joy and the most terrible hate. She stood there, smiling at me.

Then I ran from her, back to my room, tripping and nearly falling over my long skirt.

Clarice was waiting for me in my bedroom. She had heard what had happened. When she saw my face, Clarice started to cry.

'It doesn't matter, Clarice,' I said. 'Help me take off this dress. Quickly.'

'What will you wear, Madam?' Clarice asked me.

'I don't know,' I said. 'Leave me alone now. I'll be all right. Go down and enjoy the party. Don't tell anyone what has happened.'

After Clarice had gone, someone knocked at the door. It opened and Beatrice came in.

'My dear,' she said, 'are you all right?'

I put a hand up to my head and took off the wig.

'Of course I knew at once that it was a mistake,' Beatrice said. 'You could not have known.'

'Known what?' I said, turning to look at her.

'Why, about your costume. It was exactly what Rebecca wore at the last Fancy Dress Ball here. As you stood on the stairs, I thought for one terrible moment. . .'

'I ought to have known,' I said.

I was thinking of Mrs Danvers. She had planned this. She had known what would happen.

'How could you know?' said Beatrice. 'But it was a terrible shock to Maxim. He thinks that you did it as a joke. He thinks that is why you kept your dress a secret. But he will understand when you speak to him. I'm going to tell everyone that your dress didn't fit.'

I did not say anything.

'Now, what can you wear?' Beatrice said. 'Here, this blue dress is very pretty. Put this on.'

'No,' I said. 'I'm not going down.'

Beatrice stared at me before she spoke.

'But, my dear, you must. It will look so strange.'

I felt very tired.

'What does it matter?' I said.

Beatrice looked shocked at my words.

'Think of Maxim. You must come down for him,' she said.

'I can't, I can't,' I answered.

Beatrice stared at me.

'I must go down now,' she said at last. 'They will be waiting for me at dinner. I'll tell Maxim you'll be down in a minute, shall I?'

I did not answer and Beatrice walked slowly to the door and went out.

After a long time I got up from the bed where I was sitting. I walked across to the window. I could see the coloured lights in the trees. I walked back to the dressing-table and looked at my white face and red eyes in the mirror. Then slowly I washed my face and combed my hair. I put the white dress and the wig back into the box. I never wanted to see them again. I picked up the blue dress and put it on.

When I was ready, I opened the door and walked along the corridor. Everything was still and quiet. Then I heard the sound of voices. The door of the dining-room was open. The guests were coming out of dinner. Someone laughed.

I walked slowly down the stairs to meet them.

I remember very little of my first party at Manderley. It was the first and the last we ever held there. I remember that Frank tried to make me drink a little champagne. I remember Beatrice smiling at me. I remember dancing with Giles.

The band played and people danced. I stood there smiling at everyone. Maxim stood beside me. His eyes were cold and hard, not the eyes of the man I knew and loved. All through that long night, Maxim never looked at me.

Once, Beatrice came up to me and said, 'Why don't you sit down? You look like death.'

What was the time? I did not know. The night passed, hour after hour. Then at last Giles came up to me and said, 'Come and look at the fireworks on the terrace.'

I remember standing on the terrace and staring up at the sky. The fireworks rose into the sky and turned into stars and flowers. The sky was red and gold. Every window of the house was coloured by the falling lights. The grey walls of Manderley looked heavy and dark.

Then suddenly, the sky was dark too. The fireworks were over. I heard the sound of cars starting in the drive. 'They're beginning to go,' I thought. 'Thank God, they're beginning to go.'

People came up to me to say goodbye.

'Such a wonderful party,' they said. 'Thank you so much for a wonderful evening. The best party I've been to for a long time.'

I shook hands with them all. I smiled.

'I'm so glad, so glad,' I said. I could think of no other words.

Maxim had gone with Frank to stand in the drive. Beatrice came up to me.

'Well done, my dear,' she said. 'The Ball was a great success. No one had any idea about. . .you know. You must go to bed now. You look very tired. Have your breakfast in bed.'

'Yes. Yes, perhaps I shall,' I said.

'I'll tell Maxim you've gone up to bed, shall I?'

'Yes, please, Beatrice.'

The fireworks rose into the sky and turned into stars and flowers.

'All right, my dear. Sleep well.'

I walked slowly into the house. The lights had been turned off. The rooms were empty. I went up the stairs and along the corridor to my room. It was almost light now and a bird had started to sing. I undressed slowly and got into bed. I lay back and closed my eyes.

My body was tired, but my mind would not rest. I wondered how long Maxim would be. The little clock by my bed ticked away the minutes. I lay on my side, watching it. An hour went by. But Maxim did not come.

16
'Why Don't You Jump?'

I fell asleep at about seven o'clock. When I woke up again, it was after eleven. Clarice had brought me some tea. It was cold now, but I drank it. Maxim's bed was empty. He had not come to bed at all. I sat up, looking straight in front of me.

My marriage was a failure. It had failed after only three months. I was too young for Maxim, I knew too little about the world. The fact that I loved him made no difference. It was not the sort of love he needed. Maxim was not in love with me. He had never loved me. He did not belong to me, he belonged to Rebecca. Rebecca was the real Mrs de Winter.

I could never be the mistress of Manderley. Wherever I walked, wherever I sat, I saw Rebecca. I knew her well. I knew her tall, slim figure, her small face and clear white skin. If I ever heard her voice, I would know it. Rebecca – always Rebecca. I would never escape from Rebecca. She was too strong for me.

I got out of bed and opened the curtains. Sunlight filled the room. I could not hide in my bedroom any longer. I had a bath, dressed and went downstairs. The servants had been very busy. The rooms were clean and tidy. The flowers had gone. Soon there would be nothing to remind us of the Fancy Dress Ball.

I met Robert in the dining-room.

'Good morning, Robert,' I said. 'Have you seen Mr de Winter anywhere?'

'He went out soon after breakfast, Madam. He has not been in since.'

I went into the small room behind the library and picked up the telephone. Perhaps Maxim was with Frank. I had to talk to Maxim. I had to explain about last night.

'Frank, it's me,' I said when he answered. 'Where's Maxim?'

'I don't know. I haven't seen him,' Frank said. 'How did he sleep? How was he at breakfast?'

'Frank,' I said slowly, 'Maxim did not come to bed last night.'

There was silence.

'I was afraid something like that would happen,' Frank said at last.

'Where do you think he's gone?' I asked. 'I must see him. I've got to explain about last night. Maxim thinks I did it as a joke.'

I could not stop my tears now. They poured down my face as I spoke.

'You mustn't talk like that,' Frank said. 'Let me come up and see you.'

'No,' I said. 'It has happened. Nothing can be changed now. Perhaps that's a good thing. I understand things more clearly now.'

'What do you mean?' said Frank, quickly.

'Maxim doesn't love me, he loves Rebecca,' I said. 'He's never forgotten her. He's never loved me, Frank. It's always Rebecca, Rebecca, Rebecca.'

I heard Frank cry out.

'I've got to come and see you,' he said.

84

I put down the telephone and stood up. I did not want to see Frank. He could not help me. No one could help me, but myself.

Perhaps I would never see Maxim again. Perhaps Maxim had left me and would never come back. I could not get these thoughts out of my mind.

I went to the window and looked out. A fog had come up from the sea. I could not see the woods. It was very hot, but the sun was hidden behind the wall of fog. I could hear the sea and I could smell it in the fog. I walked out of the house and on to the lawn. I looked back at the house. One of the shutters in the west wing had been pulled back. Someone was standing there, looking down at me. For a moment, I thought that it was Maxim. Then the figure moved and I saw that it was Mrs Danvers.

I felt that she knew about my tears. She had planned all this to happen. This was her triumph[6] – hers and Rebecca's.

I remembered Mrs Danvers smiling at me, like a devil. But she was a living woman like myself. She was not dead, like Rebecca. I could not speak to Rebecca, but I could speak to Mrs Danvers.

I walked back across the lawn. I went through the house, along the dark silent corridor of the west wing to Rebecca's room. I turned the handle of the door and went inside.

Mrs Danvers was still standing by the window. The shutter was folded back. She turned to me and I saw that her eyes were red with crying. There were dark shadows on her white face.

'You've done what you wanted, Mrs Danvers,' I said. 'You wanted this to happen, didn't you? Are you pleased now? Are you happy?'

She turned her head away from me.

'Why did you ever come to Manderley?' she said. 'Nobody wanted you. We were all right until you came.'

'You seem to forget that I love Mr de Winter,' I said.

'If you loved him, you would never have married him,' Mrs Danvers said.

'Why do you hate me?' I asked. 'What have I done to you?'

'You tried to take Mrs de Winter's place,' she said.

'But I changed nothing here. I left everything to you. I wanted to be friends with you,' I said.

She did not answer.

'Many people marry twice,' I said. 'My marriage to Mr de Winter isn't a crime. Haven't we a right to be happy?'

'Mr de Winter is not happy,' Mrs Danvers said, looking at me at last. 'Look into his eyes. He's in hell. He has looked like that ever since she died.'

'It's not true,' I said. 'It's not true. He was happy when we were in Italy together.'

'Well, he's a man, isn't he?' she said with a hard laugh. 'Every man likes to enjoy his honeymoon.'

I was suddenly very angry and not afraid of Mrs Danvers any more. I went up to her and shook her by the arm.

'How dare you speak to me like that? How dare you? You made me wear that dress last night. You wanted to hurt Mr de Winter. Do you think his pain and unhappiness will bring Mrs de Winter back?'

Mrs Danvers moved away from me.

'What do I care for his pain?' she said. 'He's never cared about mine. How do you think I've felt, watching you sit in her place, using the things she used? I hear the servants calling you Mrs de Winter. And all the time, the real Mrs de Winter, with her smile and her lovely face is lying cold and dead in the church.'

Mrs Danvers' face was twisted with pain. Her voice was loud and hard.

'Mr de Winter deserves his pain, marrying a young girl like you – and only ten months afterwards. Well, he's paying for it now. He knows she is watching him. My lady comes at night and watches him.

'I looked after her when she was a child. Did you know that?'

'No,' I said, 'no. What's the use of this, Mrs Danvers? I don't want to hear any more.'

Mrs Danvers did not seem to hear me. She went on speaking in a high, harsh voice.

'Mrs de Winter was a lovely child,' she said. 'When she was only twelve years old, the men could not stop looking at her. But even then, she cared for nothing and nobody. And that's how she was when she grew up. She was beaten in the end. But it wasn't a man. It wasn't a woman. The sea got her. The sea was too strong for her in the end.'

Mrs Danvers began to cry noisily, with her mouth open and her eyes dry.

'Mrs Danvers, you're not well. You ought to be in bed,' I said.

She looked at me angrily.

'Leave me alone. Why shouldn't I cry? What's it to do³ with you? You came here and thought you could take Mrs de Winter's place. You! Why, even the servants laughed at you when you came to Manderley.'

'You'd better stop this, Mrs Danvers,' I said. 'You'd better go to your room.'

'Yes. And then what will you do? You'll go to Mr de Winter and tell him that Mrs Danvers has been unkind to you. You'll go to him like you did when Mr Favell came here.

'Mr de Winter was jealous of Mr Favell when she was alive. He's jealous now. That shows you he's not forgotten her, doesn't it? Of course Mr de Winter was jealous. She didn't care. She only laughed. All the men fell in love with her, Mr de Winter, Mr Favell, Mr Crawley. It was like a game to her.'

'I don't want to know,' I said. 'I don't want to know.'

Mrs Danvers came close to me and put her face near to mine.

'It's no use, is it?' she said. 'She's the real Mrs de Winter, not you.'

I backed away from her, towards the window. She took my hand and held it.

'Why don't you go?' she said again. 'He doesn't want you, he never did. He can't forget her. He wants to be alone in the house again, with her.'

She pushed me towards the open window. I could see the stones of the terrace below. Beyond the terrace was a white wall of fog.

'Look down there,' Mrs Danvers said. 'It's easy, isn't it? Why don't you jump? It wouldn't hurt. It's not like drowning. Why don't you try it? Why don't you go?'

The fog came in through the open window, damp and thick. I held on to the window ledge[1] with both hands.

'Don't be afraid,' said Mrs Danvers. 'I won't push you. You can jump. You're not happy. Mr de Winter doesn't love you. Why don't you jump now?'

The fog was thicker than before. There was fog below and all around me. If I jumped now, I would not see the stones. The fall would kill me. Maxim did not love me.

'Go on,' whispered Mrs Danvers. 'Go on, don't be afraid.'

I shut my eyes. My fingers ached from holding the ledge. The thick fog made me forget my unhappiness. I could forget about loving Maxim. I could forget about Rebecca. I would not have to think about Rebecca any more. . .

A loud explosion shook the window where we stood. The glass cracked. I opened my eyes and stared at Mrs Danvers. The first explosion was followed by another, then a third and a fourth.

'What is it?' I said. 'What has happened?'

Mrs Danvers let go my arm. She stared out of the window into the fog.

'It's the rockets[5],' she said. 'There must be a ship in trouble in the bay.'

We listened, staring into the white fog together. And then we heard the sound of footsteps on the terrace below us.

'Why don't you jump?'

17

'Rebecca Has Won'

It was Maxim down on the terrace. I could not see him, but I could hear his voice. I heard Frith answer from the hall.

'A ship's hit the rocks in the bay,' Maxim called out. 'The fog is terrible out there. Tell Mrs Danvers to have food and drink ready for the men. I'm going back to the bay to see if I can do anything.'

Mrs Danvers moved back from the window.

'We had better go down,' she said in her usual voice. 'Frith will be looking for me. Be careful of your hands. I am going to close the window.'

Then she went to the door and held it open for me.

'When you see Mr de Winter, Madam, please tell him there will be a hot meal ready for the men at any time.'

I stared at her.

'Yes,' I said. 'Yes, Mrs Danvers.'

She turned her back on me and went along the corridor. I walked slowly out of the room. I felt as though I had just woken up from a long sleep. When I reached the hall, I saw Frith.

'Did you hear the rockets, Madam?' he said. 'Mr de Winter's gone down to the bay. He went across the lawn only a few minutes ago.'

I went out on to the terrace. The fog was beginning to clear and I could see the woods again. I looked up at the window above my head. It looked very high. I suddenly felt very hot. My head ached and my hands were wet. I stood very still. Then for the first time I realized that Maxim had not gone away. I had heard his voice and he was down there in the bay. Maxim was safe. Nothing else mattered if Maxim was safe.

I began to walk along the path through the woods. The fog had almost gone now. When I came to the bay, I could see the ship at once. She was on the rocks about two miles from the shore. There were some small boats near her.

I climbed up the path to the cliffs above the bay. Frank was there talking to a coast-guard[5], but I could not see Maxim.

'They're going to send a diver[5] down soon, Mrs de Winter,' said the coastguard. 'They want to see if they can get the ship off the rocks.'

'Have you seen Maxim?' I asked Frank.

'He's taken one of the sailors to hospital,' Frank told me. 'The man was hurt. Maxim is always a great help at times like this. What are you going to do? Can I walk back with you to the house?'

'I think I'll stay here. I want to see the diver go down,' I said.

'Very well,' Frank said. 'I shall be at the office if you want me.'

The coastguard looked at his watch.

'Well, I must be getting along too,' he said. 'Good afternoon.'

The sea was calm now. The diver went down and came up again. Nothing else happened. It was very hot. I sat on the cliffs for a long time doing nothing, thinking of nothing.

When I looked at my watch again, it was three o'clock. I got up and walked down the hill to the bay. When I came to the other side, I saw Ben. He stood there, smiling at me.

'Seen the big ship?' he said.

'Yes,' I said. 'She's on the rocks, isn't she?'

'She'll break up[5],' he said. 'The big ship won't go down like the little one. She won't come back, will she?'

'Who?' I asked him.

'Her,' he said. 'The other one.'

I did not know what Ben meant. I left him and walked towards the path through the woods. I did not look at the cottage. As I went up the path, a strange fear began to fill my heart.

The house looked very peaceful. Manderley was a place of

When I came to the bay, I could see the ship at once.

safety and looked more beautiful than I had ever seen it. I felt, for the first time, that it was my home. I belonged to Manderley and Manderley belonged to me.

I went through the house and into the library. Jasper was not there. He must have gone out with Maxim. I suddenly felt very hungry, and so I asked Robert to bring in the tea. I still had a strange feeling of fear in my heart. I felt that I was waiting for something – something terrible.

As I sat drinking my tea, Robert came back into the room.

'Captain Searle, the harbour-master[5], is on the phone, Madam,' he told me. 'He wants to come here and speak to Mr de Winter at once. He says it's very important.'

'Mr de Winter is not back yet, Robert,' I told him. 'Ask Captain Searle to come up and wait.'

Robert went out of the room with the message. I wondered what Captain Searle wanted to say. It must be something to do with the ship out in the bay. But why did he want to see Maxim?

Captain Searle came into the library about fifteen minutes later. He looked at me with his bright blue eyes.

'I'm afraid I've got some bad news for Mr de Winter. I don't know how to tell him.'

'What sort of news, Captain Searle?' I asked him.

'Well, Mrs de Winter, it's not very pleasant. When we sent the diver down to look at the ship, he found something else. It was a little sailing boat. It's the boat that belonged to the late Mrs de Winter.'

'I'm sorry,' I said. 'Must you tell Mr de Winter? Can't the boat be left there?'

'The man found something else,' Captain Searle answered slowly. 'The cabin[5] door was closed, so he broke a window and looked in. Then he got a terrible fright. There was a body in there on the cabin floor. I must tell your husband, Mrs de Winter. The police will have to know too.'

This was the reason for the strange fear in my heart. Someone had been in the boat with Rebecca that night.

'Do we have to tell him?' I asked.

'I've got to do my duty,' Captain Searle said. He stopped. The door had opened. It was Maxim.

'Hello,' he said. 'Is something the matter, Captain Searle?'

I felt very afraid. I went out of the room quickly and shut the door behind me. Jasper was in the hall and he walked out on to the terrace with me. I sat down. I must not fail Maxim now.

I sat on the terrace until I heard Captain Searle's car drive away. Then I stood up and walked slowly back to the library.

Maxim was standing by the window. I went and stood beside him. I took his hand and held it against my face.

'I want to help you, Maxim,' I said. 'I've grown up, you know. I'm not a child any more.'

Maxim put his arm round me and held me closely.

'I was angry with you last night, wasn't I?' he said.

'Maxim,' I asked him, 'can't we start again?'

'It's too late, my darling, too late,' he said. 'We've lost our chance of happiness. Something has happened. Something I've dreamt about, night after night. I knew we could never be happy.'

Maxim held both my hands and looked into my face.

'Rebecca has won,' he said.

I stared at him. My heart began to beat fast. What was Maxim trying to tell me?

'I always knew this would happen,' Maxim said. 'Rebecca has kept us apart all this time. I remember how she looked at me before she died. I remember her smile. She knew this would happen. She knew she would win in the end.'

'Maxim,' I whispered. 'What are you trying to tell me? Captain Searle told me about the boat. There was someone sailing with Rebecca. You have to find out who it was. That's it, isn't it, Maxim?'

'No,' he said. 'you don't understand. There was no one with Rebecca. She was alone.'

I stood there watching his face, watching his eyes.

'It's Rebecca's body lying there on the cabin floor.'

'No,' I said. 'No!'

'The woman buried in the church is not Rebecca. I always knew that,' Maxim said. 'Rebecca was not drowned. I killed her. I shot Rebecca in the cottage. I carried her body to the cabin, took the boat out that night and sank it. It's Rebecca who's lying there on the cabin floor. Will you look into my eyes and tell me that you love me now?'

18

The Truth About Rebecca

It was very quiet in the library. When people have a great shock, they feel nothing at first. I stood beside Maxim and I had no feelings at all. Then Maxim took me in his arms and began to kiss me. I shut my eyes. He had never kissed me like this before.

'I love you so much,' he whispered.

This is what I had wanted him to say, every day and every night. But I could feel nothing now.

Maxim stopped suddenly and pushed me away from him.

'You see, I was right,' he said. 'It's too late. You don't love me now.'

'It's not too late,' I said, putting my arms round him. 'I love you more than anything in the world.'

'It's no use now,' said Maxim. 'We have no time. They've found the boat. They've found Rebecca.'

I stared at him, not understanding.

'What will they do?' I said.

'They will make sure that the body in the cabin is Rebecca. Then they will remember that other body in the church. The other woman – the one I said was Rebecca.'

'What are we going to do?' I said.

Maxim did not answer.

'Does anyone know? Anyone at all?' I said.

Maxim shook his head.

'Are you sure Frank doesn't know?' I asked quickly.

'How could he?' said Maxim. 'There was nobody there but me. It was dark. . .' He stopped. He sat down on a chair and I went and knelt beside him.

'Why didn't you tell me?' I whispered.

'I nearly did, once,' Maxim said. 'But you always seemed so unhappy and so shy.'

I answered very quietly.

'I knew you were thinking about Rebecca all the time. How could I ask you to love me when I knew you loved Rebecca?'

'You thought I loved Rebecca?' he said. 'I hated her. We never loved each other. Rebecca never loved anyone except herself.'

I sat on the floor, staring at him.

'She was clever of course,' Maxim went on. ' Everyone thought she was the kindest, the most charming person. When I married her, people told me I was the luckiest man in the world.'

'I found out the truth five days after we were married. We were in the hills near Monte Carlo. It was the same place I went to with you. Do you remember? She sat there in the car and told me terrible, evil things about herself. Things that I could not tell anyone.'

Maxim stared out of the window.

'I did not kill her then,' he said. 'I let her laugh. She knew that I would take her to Manderley. She knew I would never divorce[4] her. I would never tell people all the terrible things she had told me.'

Maxim came up to me and held out his hands.

'You hate me, don't you?' he said. 'You can't understand me, can you?'

I did not say anything. I held his hands against my heart. Only one thing mattered. Maxim did not love Rebecca. He had never loved her, never, never.

Maxim was talking again.

'I thought about Manderley too much,' he said. 'I put Manderley first, before anything else. I can't tell you about those terrible years with Rebecca. But she made Manderley the place of beauty it is today. And I accepted everything, because of Manderley.

'Rebecca was careful at first,' Maxim went on. 'She had a flat in London. She met her friends there. Then she began to grow careless. She invited friends down here, to Manderley. I warned her. I told her that Manderley was mine. Rebecca did not say anything. She only smiled.

'Then Frank came to me and told me he wanted to leave. He wouldn't say why at first. But I got the truth from him in the end. Rebecca never left him alone. She was always going to his house and asking him to her cottage.

'Rebecca went up to London for a time. When she came back, she took Giles out sailing with her. I knew what had happened as soon as they came back. Beatrice and Giles never stayed at Manderley again. After that, I knew I could never trust Rebecca with anyone.

'She had a cousin, an awful man, called Jack Favell. He started to come here when I was away.'

'I've met him,' I said. 'He came here the day you went to London. I didn't tell you. I didn't want to remind you of Rebecca.'

'Remind me?' said Maxim. 'Oh God, I never needed to be reminded.

'Favell often stayed with Rebecca down at the cottage. He is a bad man. He's been in trouble with the police many times. I told Rebecca that I would shoot Favell if he came to Manderley again.

'Then, one night, I could stand our life here no longer. Rebecca came back from London very late. She went to the cottage. I thought Favell was with her. I went after them. I took a gun to frighten him.'

Maxim was talking in quick, short sentences. I held his hand tightly.

'I saw a light in the cottage and went in. To my surprise, Rebecca was alone. She looked ill and strange.

' "This is the end," I told her. "I can't stand any more." Rebecca looked at me and smiled.

' "It won't be easy to divorce me," she said. "Everyone believes our marriage is perfect."

'Then she stood up and walked towards me.

' "If I had a child, Max," she said, "Everyone would think it was yours. You would like a son, wouldn't you? A boy to grow up at Manderley. And you would never know who his father was."

'And she smiled at me again. She was smiling when I killed her. The bullet went through her heart.'

Maxim's voice was very low. He spoke slowly.

'There was blood all over the floor. I had to get water from the sea to clean the place.

'There was no moon and it was very dark,' Maxim went on. 'I carried Rebecca's body to the boat. I laid the body on the floor of the cabin. Then I took the boat out into the bay. I wanted to take the boat a good way out, but the wind was too strong for me.

'I made some holes in the wooden planks with a metal spike. I opened the sea cocks[5] and the sea water flowed in. In a few minutes it had covered my feet. I shut the cabin door behind me, climbed into the dinghy[5] and rowed back. Rebecca's boat was already sinking. I sat and watched it go down.'

Maxim looked at me.

'I made some holes in the wooden planks with a metal spike.'

'That's all,' he said. 'There's no more to tell.'

The library was very quiet. We sat there together for some minutes without saying anything. Then Maxim began to speak again.

'I knew the boat would be found one day,' he said. 'Rebecca knew she would win in the end. I saw her smile when she died.'

'But Rebecca is dead,' I told him. 'That's what we must remember.'

'The diver has seen the body. They're going to get the boat up tomorrow morning. They'll find out that it's Rebecca's body in the cabin.'

'Then you must say you made a mistake about the other body. Nobody saw you that night. We are the only two people who know what happened that night, Maxim.'

'Yes,' he said. 'Yes, I suppose so.'

'They will think the boat sank when Rebecca went down into the cabin. They'll think she was trapped there. They'll think that, won't they, Maxim?' I said.

'I don't know,' Maxim replied slowly. 'I don't know.'

At that moment, the telephone in the next room began to ring.

19

Colonel Julyan

Maxim went into the little room and closed the door. I sat there, listening to the sound of Maxim's voice. I was no longer afraid of Rebecca; I did not hate her any more. Maxim and I were going to fight this together. Rebecca had not won, she had lost.

'That was Colonel Julyan,' said Maxim, as he came back into

the room. He is the local magistrate[4]. He has to be there when they get the boat up tomorrow. He asked me if I had made a mistake about the other body.'

The telephone began to ring again. Maxim answered it quickly and came back into the library.

'It's begun,' he said.

'What do you mean?' asked.

'That was a reporter. The whole thing will be in the papers tomorrow. There's nothing we can do.'

After dinner, we went back into the library as usual. I sat at Maxim's feet, my head against his knees. In a strange way, we were completely happy.

Rain fell in the night. When I woke up in the morning, Maxim had already gone out. I went down to breakfast as usual. There were a lot of letters thanking us for the Ball. How far away that seemed! I felt calmer, much older now. I took the letters into the morning-room. To my surprise, the room was dusty and untidy. The windows were tightly closed and some of the flowers were dead. I rang the bell for a maid and when she came, I spoke to her angrily. I wondered why I had been frightened of the servants before.

The menu for the day lay on the desk. It was the same food as the day before. I crossed everything out and rang for Robert.

'Tell Mrs Danvers to order something different,' I told him. Then I went out into the garden and cut some roses. Very soon Maxim will be back, I thought. I must be calm and quiet. I took the roses back into the morning-room. It was clean and tidy now.

As I began to arrange the flowers, there was a knock at the door.

It was Mrs Danvers, holding the menu in her hand. She looked pale and tired.

'I don't understand,' she said. 'I'm not used to having messages sent by Robert. When Mrs de Winter wanted any change in the menu, she spoke to me herself.'

'I am Mrs de Winter now, Mrs Danvers,' I said. 'And I shall do things in my own way.'

Mrs Danvers stared at me.

'Is it true,' she asked slowly, 'that Mrs de Winter's boat has been found and that there was a body in the cabin?'

'I am afraid I don't know anything about that,' I said.

'Don't you?' Mrs Danvers said. She stood looking at me. I turned away.

'I will give orders about the lunch,' she said. She waited, but I did not say anything. She went out of the room.

Mrs Danvers did not frighten me any more. She was my enemy and I did not care. But if she learnt the truth about Rebecca's death, she would become Maxim's enemy too. I suddenly felt sick and ill. I went out on to the terrace and began to walk up and down.

At half past eleven, Maxim phoned me from Frank's office. He told me he was bringing Colonel Julyan and Frank back for lunch.

The time dragged by. At five to one, I heard the sound of a car in the drive. Maxim came into the hall with Frank and Colonel Julyan.

Colonel Julyan, the magistrate, was a middle-aged man with a kind face and grey hair.

'This is most unpleasant for you and your husband,' Colonel Julyan said to me. 'I feel very sorry for both of you.'

Maxim and Frank went on into the dining-room and Colonel Julyan continued to speak to me quietly.

'We found a body in the boat this morning. It is the body of the late Mrs de Winter. As you know, Mr de Winter identified the other body found in the sea as his wife. That makes things rather difficult for us now.'

The Colonel stopped suddenly as Maxim came back into the hall.

'Lunch is ready; shall we go in?' he said.

I did not look at Maxim during lunch. We talked about the weather and Colonel Julyan asked me about my life in France. Frith and Robert were in the room and no one wanted to talk about the boat. At last Frith served coffee and the servants left us.

'I wish an inquest[4] wasn't necessary,' Colonel Julyan said. 'but I'm afraid it is. I don't think it will take very long. De Winter will have to say that the body in the boat was the late Mrs de Winter. Then the boat-builder will say that the boat was in good order when he last saw it. This must be done.'

'That's quite all right,' Maxim said. 'We understand.'

'I suppose Mrs de Winter had to go down into the cabin for something. Then the door shut and, somehow, she was trapped there. Don't you think so, Crawley?' the Colonel asked Frank.

'Oh yes, of course,' said Frank. I had a sudden feeling that Frank knew the truth.

'The inquest will be on Tuesday afternoon,' Colonel Julyan told us. 'We'll keep it as short as possible, but I'm afraid the reporters will be there.'

There was another silence.

'Shall we go into the garden?' I said.

We all stood on the terrace for a moment and then Colonel Julyan looked at his watch.

'Thank you for the lunch,' he said to me. 'I'm afraid I must leave now. Would you like a lift, Crawley?'

Maxim walked with them to the car. When they had gone, he came back to me on the terrace.

'It's going to be all right,' Maxim said. 'There won't be any trouble at the inquest. There is nothing to show what I did. Colonel Julyan thinks she was trapped in the cabin and the jury will think that too.'

I said nothing.

'It's you I'm sorry for,' Maxim told me sadly. 'I don't care about anything else. I'm glad that I killed Rebecca. But I can't forget what this has done to you. You have lost that young, sweet look. And it will never come back. In twenty-four hours, you have grown so much older.'

Frith brought in the newspapers at breakfast the following day. The story was in all of them. There was a picture of Manderley and an awful one of Maxim. All the papers said that Rebecca's body had been found after the Fancy Dress Ball. They said how everyone had loved Rebecca. They all said that Maxim had married his young, second wife within a year of Rebecca's death. It all made a good story. Maxim's face went whiter and whiter.

I wondered what the papers would say if they knew the truth. That terrible word – murder – would be on every front page.

Frank was a great help to us. We had no more phone calls from reporters and no visitors. It was just a question of waiting – of waiting until Tuesday.

Maxim and I stayed quietly in the house or in the gardens. We did not walk in the woods or go down to the sea. The weather was very hot and the air was heavy. There were clouds, but the rain did not fall.

20

The Inquest

Tuesday came at last. The inquest was at two o'clock. After an early lunch, I drove into the town with Maxim.

'I think I shall stay here in the car,' I said. 'I won't come in with you after all.'

'I didn't want you to come,' Maxim said. 'I wish you had stayed at Manderley.'

Maxim went off and left me sitting there. The minutes went by. I wondered what was happening at the inquest. I got out of the car and began walking up and down.

A policeman looked at me.

'Excuse me, Madam,' he said. 'Aren't you Mrs de Winter? You can wait inside if you like.'

The policeman took me into an empty room. Five minutes passed. Nothing happened. I got up and walked out of the little room. The policeman was still standing there.

'How long will they be?' I asked him.

'I'll go and see if you like,' the policeman said. He was back again in a moment.

'It won't last much longer,' he told me. 'Mr de Winter has just finished giving his evidence[4]. There's only the boat-builder, Mr Tabb, to speak now. Would you like to go in? There's an empty seat near the door.'

I followed the policeman. He opened the door for me and I went in quietly and sat down. The room was small and full of people. The air was hot and stuffy. Frank was sitting next to Maxim. To my surprise, Mrs Danvers was there too, with Favell beside her. I wondered whether Maxim had seen him.

Tabb, the boat-builder, standing in the centre of the room, was answering the Coroner's[4] questions.

'Was the boat in good condition?' the Coroner was asking.

'Yes, it certainly was the last time I saw it,' Tabb said. 'It was a strong little boat. I can't understand why it sank that night.'

'Accidents have happened before,' the Coroner said. 'Mrs de Winter was careless for a moment and she died.'

'Excuse me, sir,' said the boat-builder. 'I would like to say something else.'

'Very well, go on,' said the Coroner.

'It's this, sir. There was nothing wrong with that boat when I last saw it. So what I want to know is this. Who made those holes in the planks? Rocks didn't do it. The boat sank too far away from

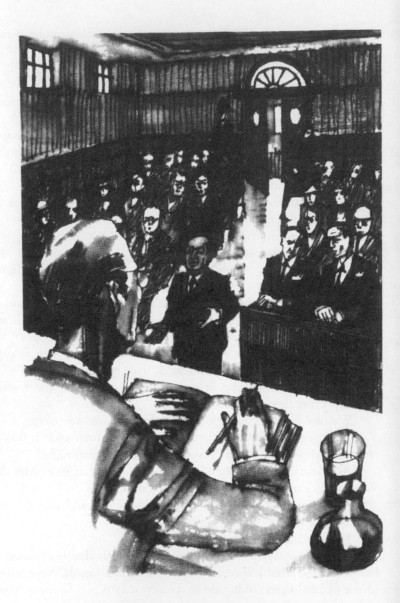

Tabb, the boat-builder, was answering the Coroner's questions.

them. And those holes were made with something sharp.'

I could not look at anyone. I stared down at the floor.

For a moment, the Coroner was too surprised to speak. Then he said, 'What do you mean? What sort of holes?'

'There were three of them, in different parts of the boat. And that's not all. The sea-cocks had been turned full on.'

'The sea-cocks? What are they?' asked the Coroner.

'The sea-cocks close the pipes leading to the wash-basins, sir. They must be kept tightly closed when the boat is sailing. Otherwise the sea water comes in.'

It was hot in that crowded room, far too hot. I wished someone would open a window. The boat-builder was speaking again.

'With those holes, sir, and the sea-cocks open, a small boat like Mrs de Winter's would soon sink. It's my opinion that there was no accident. That boat was sunk on purpose.'

I must try and get out of the door, I thought. There was no air. People were standing up and talking loudly. I heard the Coroner say, 'Mr de Winter.'

Maxim was standing up. I could not look at him.

'Mr de Winter,' the Coroner said, 'you have heard James Tabb's evidence. Do you know anything about those holes?'

'Nothing.'

'Can you think why they are there?'

'No, of course not.'

'This news is a shock to you, of course?'

'Of course it is a shock. Does it surprise you that I am shocked?'

Maxim's voice was hard and angry.

Oh God, I thought, don't let Maxim lose his temper.

The Coroner was speaking again.

'Mr de Winter, I want to find out exactly how your late wife died. Who looked after Mrs de Winter's boat?'

'She looked after it herself.'

'Then whoever took the boat out that night also made those holes and opened the sea-cocks.'

'I suppose so.'

'You have told us that the door and windows of the cabin were shut?'

'Yes.'

'Doesn't this seem very strange to you, Mr de Winter?'

'Yes, it does.'

'Mr de Winter, I'm afraid I must ask you one other question. Were you and the late Mrs de Winter happily married?'

It was hot, so hot. I tried to stand up, but I could not. The ground came up to meet me. And then I heard Maxim's voice, clear and strong.

'Will someone take my wife outside? She is going to faint.'

———

I was sitting in the little room again. Frank was beside me.

'I'm sorry,' I said. 'It was so hot in there.'

'Are you feeling better, Mrs de Winter?' Frank asked. 'Maxim has told me to take you back to Manderley.' Frank helped me to get up.

'I'd much rather stay,' I said. 'I want to wait for Maxim.'

'Maxim may be some time,' Frank told me. 'They may have to go over the evidence again.'

'But what are they trying to find out?'

Frank did not answer. We were in his car now and he was driving very fast.

'Did you see Favell there?' I asked. 'He was sitting with Mrs Danvers. I don't trust them, Frank. They might make trouble.'

Frank did not answer. He could not know how much Maxim had told me. Then we were back at Manderley.

'Will you be all right now?' Frank asked me. 'I shall go back. Maxim may want me.' He got quickly back into the car again and drove away.

I went upstairs to my room and lay down on my bed. What were they all saying now? What was happening? What would I do if Frank came back to Manderley without Maxim? I thought again of that dreadful word – murder. God, let me not think about it. Let me think about something else, anything . . .

I must have fallen asleep. I woke up suddenly. It was five o'clock. I got up and went to the window. There was no wind. Lightning flashed against the grey sky. I heard thunder in the distance. A few drops of rain began to fall.

I went downstairs and sat with Jasper in the library.

21

A Visit From Jack Favell

It was after six when I heard the sound of Maxim's car. I tried to stand up but my legs were so weak that I had to lean against a chair. Maxim came into the room and stood by the door. He looked tired and old.

'It's all over,' he said. I waited. I could not speak or walk towards him.

'Suicide,' Maxim said. 'That's the verdict[4]. They said that Rebecca killed herself.'

I sat down. 'Suicide,' I repeated. 'Why do they think Rebecca did that?'

'God knows[3],' Maxim said. He went and stood by the window. 'There's one more thing to be done. Rebecca's body has to be buried. I'm going down to the church now. We'll talk about everything when I get back. We've got to start our lives all over again. The past can't hurt us if we are together. We'll have children too, I promise you. I must go now. I'm meeting Frank and Colonel Julyan at the church.' He left the room quickly and then I heard the sound of his car driving away.

It was quiet in the library. I thought about the church where Rebecca was being buried at last.

Just before seven, the rain began to fall heavily. I opened the windows to let in the cold, clean air. The rain was falling so heavily that I did not hear Frith come in.

'Excuse me, Madam,' he said. 'There's a gentleman to see Mr de Winter. It's Mr Favell.'

I was very surprised.

'I think I had better see Mr Favell,' I said. 'Bring him in here, please, Frith.' I hoped that Favell would go before Maxim came back. I could not think why Favell had come.

'I'm afraid Maxim is not here,' I said, when Favell walked into the room. His eyes were red. I wondered if he had been drinking.

'I don't mind waiting,' Favell replied. 'Max will be back for dinner, I'm sure.'

'Mr Favell,' I said. 'I don't want to be rude, but I am very tired. It will be better if you come back in the morning.'

'No, no,' he said, coming towards me, 'I've got something to say to Max. This has been a shock to me, you know. I was very fond of Rebecca.'

'Yes, of course,' I said. 'I'm very sorry for you.'

'I was fonder of Rebecca than of anyone else in the world,' Favell went on. 'And she was fond of me. That's why I've come here to find out the truth. Suicide . . . my God. You and I know it wasn't suicide, don't we?'

As Favell was speaking, the door opened and Maxim and Frank came in.

'What the hell are you doing here?' Maxim said to Favell.

'Why, hello, Max, old man,' Favell said. 'You must be feeling very pleased with yourself.'

110

'Do you mind leaving the house?' said Maxim coldly. 'I don't want you here.'

'Now, wait a minute, Max,' Favell answered. 'You've been very lucky. But I can still make life unpleasant for you. And dangerous too, perhaps.' Maxim stared hard at Favell.

'Oh yes?' he said. 'In what way can you make things dangerous?'

'I'll tell you, Max,' said Favell with an unpleasant smile. 'You know all about Rebecca and me. Her death was a great shock. Then I read about Rebecca's boat and the body in the cabin. So I went to the inquest. I heard the boat-builder's evidence. What about those holes in the boat, Max?'

'You heard the verdict,' Maxim told him. 'I have nothing more to say.' Favell laughed.

'You know Rebecca didn't kill herself. I've a note here that may interest you. I kept it because it was the last thing Rebecca ever wrote to me. Listen.'

Favell took a piece of paper from his pocket. I recognized Rebecca's hard, black writing.

' "I tried to phone you," Favell read, "but you were out. I'm leaving London now and going back to Manderley. I'll wait for you in the cottage. Come down as soon as you can. I've got something to tell you." '

Favell put the note back in his pocket.

'I found that in my London flat. It was too late to drive down to Manderley. When I phoned the following day, Rebecca was dead. Do you really think Rebecca killed herself after writing that note?'

Maxim said nothing.

'Now, Max, old man,' Favell said at last, 'you know I'm not a rich man. If I had two or three thousand pounds, I could live quite well. I'd never come back, I promise you.'

'I've already asked you to leave the house,' Maxim said. 'The door is behind you.'

Favell laughed again.

111

'Think again, Max,' said Favell. 'I don't suppose your new bride wants to be known as the wife of a murderer.'

'You can't frighten me, Favell,' Maxim answered. 'Shall I phone Colonel Julyan? You can tell your story to him.'

'You wouldn't dare, Max,' said Favell. 'I have enough evidence to hang[4] you, Max.'

Maxim walked slowly towards the telephone in the next room.

'Stop him,' I said to Frank. 'Stop him for God's sake.' But it was too late. Maxim was already speaking.

'Is that Colonel Julyan? It's de Winter here. Could you come over to Manderley at once? No – I can't say anything over the phone. Thank you very much, goodbye.'

Maxim came back again into the room.

'Colonel Julyan will be here in ten minutes,' he said.

We waited in silence. The rain was so heavy that we did not hear the sound of the car. We were taken by surprise when Frith brought the magistrate into the library.

'Good evening, Colonel Julyan,' Maxim said at once. 'This is Jack Favell, my late wife's cousin. He has something to say to you.'

Favell went up to Colonel Julyan. 'I'm not happy about the verdict. I want you to read this note. Tell me whether you think the writer had decided to kill herself.' Colonel Julyan took the note and read it slowly.

'I see what you mean,' he said. 'But the note is not clear. What do you think really happened to Mrs de Winter?' Favell looked at Maxim.

'I'll tell you what I think,' he said slowly. 'Rebecca never opened those sea-cocks. She didn't make those holes in the boat. Rebecca didn't kill herself. I say she was murdered. Do you want to know who the murderer is? He's there, standing by the window. Mr Maximilian de Winter – he's your murderer. Take a good look at him.'

Favell began to laugh, a high stupid laugh, as he twisted the note round and round in his fingers.

22
Rebecca's Diary

Thank God for Favell's laugh. I saw a look of disgust come into Colonel Julyan's face.

'The man's drunk,' he said quickly. 'He doesn't know what he's saying.'

'Drunk, am I?' shouted Favell. 'Oh no, I'm not drunk. Max de Winter murdered Rebecca, and I'm going to prove it.'

'Wait a minute,' said Colonel Julyan. 'I want to hear your proof.'

'Proof?' said Favell. 'Aren't those holes in the boat enough proof for you?'

'Certainly not,' said Colonel Julyan. 'Unless you can find someone who saw him do it.'

'I'll get your proof for you,' shouted Favell. 'De Winter killed Rebecca because of me. He was jealous because she loved me. He went down to the cottage and killed her there. Wait a minute . . . I think I can find someone who saw him.'

I suddenly knew what Favell meant. Someone had seen it all happen – someone who was often down there in the bay– Ben.

'There's an idiot who was always around the cottage,' Favell said. 'He often slept on the beach. I'm sure he saw everything.'

'Can we get this man and question him?' asked Colonel Julyan.

'Of course,' said Maxim. 'His name is Ben. Could you go and get him, Frank? Take your car.' Frank went out quickly.

Favell laughed angrily. His face was very red.

'You all help each other down here, don't you?' he said. 'Crawley knows the truth, I'm sure. He'll be there to hold the young bride's arm when Max is sentenced[4] to death.'

Without warning, Maxim went up to Favell and hit him hard. Favell fell heavily to the floor. I wished that Maxim had not hit him. Favell got slowly to his feet, walked over to a small table and poured himself some whisky. I saw Colonel Julyan look thoughtfully at Maxim. Was he beginning to believe Favell's story?

The door opened and Frank came in.

'All right, Ben,' he said quietly. 'Don't be frightened.'

Ben stepped into the room and stared at everyone with his small eyes. Favell walked up to him.

'You know who I am, don't you?' he said. Ben did not answer.

'Come on,' said Favell. 'You've seen me in the cottage, haven't you?'

Ben held Frank's arm. 'I've never seen him,' he said. 'Is he going to take me away?'

'No, of course not,' said Colonel Julyan. 'Now listen to me, Ben. You remember the lady with the boat. Were you on the beach when she took her boat out for the last time?'

'You were there, weren't you?' said Favell, standing over Ben. 'You saw Mrs de Winter go into the cottage and Mr de Winter too. What happened then?'

Ben shook his head and moved back against the wall. 'I didn't see anything,' he said. He began to cry.

'You damned little idiot,' Favell said slowly.

'I think Ben can go home now, don't you, Colonel Julyan?' Maxim said. Frank took Ben out of the room as the Colonel nodded his head.

'That poor fellow was terrified,' he said. 'He's no use to you, Favell. I'm afraid you can't prove your story.'

Favell did not answer. Instead, he rang the bell and when Frith came in, he said, 'Ask Mrs Danvers to come here, Frith.'

'Isn't Mrs Danvers the housekeeper?' asked Colonel Julyan as Frith left the room.

'I've never seen him,' Ben said. 'Is he going to take me away?'

'She was also Rebecca's friend. She knew her for years,' Favell said, with his unpleasant smile.

We all waited, watching the door. Then Mrs Danvers came in and shut the door behind her.

'Good evening, Mrs Danvers,' Colonel Julyan said. 'I would like to ask you a question. You knew the late Mrs de Winter well. Mr Favell has told us that Mrs de Winter was in love with him. Is that true?'

'No, it is not,' Mrs Danvers answered.

'Now, listen, Danny,' Favell began to shout, but Mrs Danvers took no notice.

'She was not in love with you, Mr Jack. Or with Mr de Winter. She was not in love with anyone. She thought men were fools. She amused herself with you, that was all.'

Maxim went very white. Favell stared at Mrs Danvers as though he did not understand her.

'Mrs Danvers,' Colonel Julyan said quietly, 'can you think of any reason why Mrs de Winter killed herself?'

Mrs Danvers shook her head. 'No, certainly not,' she said.

'There you are! What did I tell you?' Favell shouted.

'Be quiet, will you. Let Mrs Danvers read the note. She may understand it,' Colonel Julyan said. Mrs Danvers took the note, read it and then shook her head again.

'I don't know what she meant. If it was something important, she would have told me.'

'Can you tell us how Mrs de Winter spent that last day in London? Did she keep a diary?' asked Colonel Julyan.

'I've got her diary in my room,' Mrs Danvers replied. 'I kept all her things. I'll go and get it.'

'Well, de Winter,' said Colonel Julyan, 'do you mind us seeing this diary?'

'Of course not,' said Maxim. Once again, I saw Colonel Julyan give Maxim a hard look. This time Frank saw it too. Somehow I felt sure that the truth was in that diary.

Mrs Danvers came back with a small book in her hand.

'Here is the page for the day Mrs de Winter died,' she said. Colonel Julyan looked at it carefully.

'Yes,' he said, 'here it is. Hairdressers at twelve o'clock. Then lunch. And then – Baker – two o'clock. Who was Baker?' He looked at Maxim. Maxim shook his head.

'Baker?' repeated Mrs Danvers. 'She knew no one called Baker.'

'We must find out who this person was,' said Colonel Julyan. 'If he wasn't a friend, perhaps it was someone she was afraid of.'

'Mrs de Winter afraid?' said Mrs Danvers. 'She was afraid of nothing and no one. Only one thing worried her. That was the thought of illness, of dying slowly in her bed.'

'What does all this matter?' said Favell. 'If Baker was important Danny would know about him.' Mrs Danvers was turning the pages of the diary.

'There's a telephone number here at the back,' she said. 'And the name Baker again.'

'Well,' said Maxim, lighting a cigarette. 'Perhaps someone should phone that number. Would you mind, Frank?'

Frank took the diary without a word and went into the next room. He shut the door behind him. When he came back, he said, 'That was a doctor's number. Dr Baker used to live there, but he left six months ago. They gave me his new address. I have written it here.' And Frank held out a piece of paper.

It was then that Maxim looked at me. He looked at me like a man saying goodbye for the last time. That piece of paper was enough to hang Maxim.

I knew why Rebecca had gone to a doctor. I knew what she had wanted to tell Favell. Rebecca had been pregnant when she died. She had been going to have a child. It was the one clear proof that Rebecca had not killed herself.

I was sure that this was the truth. I knew Maxim thought so too.

'Well done, Frank,' said Maxim calmly. 'Where does the doctor live now?'

'In north London,' Frank replied. 'But he's not on the phone. He's a very well-known women's doctor.'

'Well,' said Colonel Julyan. 'There must have been something wrong with her after all.'

'I'll write him a letter,' Frank said.

'I don't think he would tell you anything,' Colonel Julyan answered. 'I think de Winter should see him and explain.'

'I'm ready to go,' said Maxim quietly. 'Shall I go up in the morning?'

'He's not going alone,' Favell said with a laugh. 'You go with him, Julyan. And I think I'd better go too. What time do we start?'

Colonel Julyan looked at Maxim.

'Nine o'clock?' he said. 'Perhaps you will take me in your car.'

'We'll meet at the crossroads just after nine,' Favell said. He walked to the door.

'I suppose you're not going to ask me to dinner, so I'll say goodbye. Come on, Danny. I'll see you in the morning, Max.'

Colonel Julyan came up to me and took my hand.

'Good night,' he said. 'Get your husband to bed early. Tomorrow will be a long day.' He held my hand for a moment, but he did not look into my eyes. He and Frank went out together. Maxim and I were alone at last.

'I'm coming with you tomorrow,' I said.

'Yes,' Maxim answered. 'We must be together as long as we can.'

I put my arms around him and held him. We did not say anything. Then Maxim held me tightly. We began to kiss each other, like guilty lovers who had never kissed before.

Dr Baker

I woke up early the following morning at about six o'clock. I got up and went to the window. The trees were covered in mist. There was a sharp coolness in the air. Autumn had arrived.

This was the start of a new day at Manderley. Soon the servants would be starting work. Whatever happened to us, life at Manderley would go on. The peace of Manderley could not be broken. Its beauty could not be destroyed. The flowers would come every year, the birds would sing. Manderley would always be here, safe and secure, within sound of the sea.

Maxim slept on and I did not wake him. The day ahead would be long and tiring. London was many miles away. We did not know what we should find at the end of the journey.

Somewhere in London lived a man called Baker. He had never heard of us. But our future was in his hands.

I had a bath, dressed and then woke Maxim. He got up and went into the bathroom. I began to pack a few things. We might have to stay overnight in London. I looked at my small case. It seemed so long since I had used it. But it was only four months. I could not believe it.

We had breakfast together and I went out on to the terrace. The air was fresh and clear now. It was going to be a perfect day. At nine o'clock exactly, Frank brought up Colonel Julyan in his car.

We were going in Maxim's car. I sat beside Maxim and Colonel Julyan got into the back.

'You will telephone, won't you?' Frank said as he stood on the steps.

'Yes, of course,' Maxim said. As we drove away, I looked back at the house. It had never looked more beautiful. For some reason, my eyes filled with tears. Then we were round the bend of the drive and I could see the house no longer.

When we came to the crossroads, Favell was already waiting. He waved when he saw us and started up his car. I settled down for the long journey to London. The hours passed and the miles went by, Favell's car always behind us.

We had lunch somewhere and reached London at about three o'clock. It was then that I began to feel tired. It was warm and the streets were busy. The drive through the centre of London seemed very long. Maxim looked pale and tired, but he did not say anything. Favell's car was always behind us.

We reached Baker's house at about five o'clock. Maxim stopped the car and we got out. Favell came up to meet us. We all walked slowly up the path to the front door. Colonel Julyan rang the bell.

A woman opened the door.

'Is Dr Baker at home?' said Colonel Julyan. 'He is expecting us. I sent a telegram.'

'Yes, of course,' said the woman. 'My husband is in the garden. I'll tell him you are here.'

She took us into a cool room at the back of the house. She went out and in a few minutes a tall man came into the room.

'I'm Dr Baker. I'm sorry to keep you waiting. Please sit down,' he said.

'We are sorry to trouble you, Dr Baker,' Colonel Julyan said. 'My name is Julyan. This is Mr de Winter, Mrs de Winter and Mr Favell. We have come about the death of the late Mrs de Winter. You may have read the report in the papers.'

'The verdict was suicide,' Favell said. 'I knew Mrs de Winter very well. She did not kill herself. She had no reason to. We want to know why she came to see you on the day she died.'

Dr Baker looked surprised. 'I think you've made a mistake,' he said. 'No one called de Winter has ever come to me.'

'But we found your old telephone number in Mrs de Winter's diary.' Dr Baker looked at the page from the diary that Colonel Julyan was holding out to him.

'That certainly was my number,' he said.

'Perhaps Mrs de Winter gave you a different name,' Colonel Julyan suggested.

'It's possible,' said Dr Baker slowly.

'If you have any record of a visit on that day, could we see it?' Colonel Julyan asked. 'This is an important matter.'

'Murder,' Favell said.

'Of course,' said the doctor. 'I had no idea there was any question of that. I'll go and get my book.'

While Dr Baker was out of the room, we said nothing. No one looked at anyone else. Favell whistled quietly under his breath.

Dr Baker came back into the room with a large book. He opened the book and turned the pages. We all stood watching his face.

'I saw a Mrs Danvers on the 12th at two o'clock,' Dr Baker said at last.

'Danny? Why did. . .?' Favell began. Maxim broke in.

'Rebecca gave the wrong name, of course,' he said. 'Do you remember the visit now, Doctor?' But Dr Baker was already searching his files[6]. He picked out a card and read it.

'Yes,' he said slowly, 'I remember now.'

'Was she tall and dark, a beautiful woman?' Colonel Julyan asked.

'Yes,' said Dr Baker. He put back the card and looked at Maxim. The doctor spoke slowly.

'The woman who called herself Mrs Danvers was very ill indeed. She had come to me the week before. I took some X-rays. She had come back to hear the result. I remember her words exactly. "I want to know the truth," she said. "If I'm really ill, I want to know." So I told her.'

121

Dr Baker picked a card out of his files and read it.

Dr Baker stopped and looked down at the files.

'There was nothing to be done,' he went on. 'An operation would have been useless. I told her that. In six months, she would have been dead.'

No one said a word and the doctor went on, 'Mrs de Winter looked a healthy woman. She had very little pain at that time. But the pain would have come. The X-rays showed that she could never have had a child. But that was nothing to do with her illness.'

Everyone was standing up. We shook hands with Dr Baker and he walked with us to the front door.

'Shall I send you my report?' Dr Baker asked.

'We may not need it,' said Colonel Julyan. 'We'll write to you if we do. Thank you very much.'

'I am glad to have been of some use,' said Dr Baker. 'Goodbye.' And he shut the door.

24

The Return to Manderley

We went and stood by the car. No one said anything for a few minutes. Favell's face was grey. His hand shook as he lit a cigarette.

'She kept it a secret from everyone, even Danny. It's been a dreadful shock to me,' Favell said. 'You're all right, of course, Max. You've been lucky, haven't you? You and your young wife can go back to Manderley now. You think you've won, but don't be too sure, I haven't finished with you yet.'

'Shall we get into the car and go?' Colonel Julyan asked Maxim. Favell smiled unpleasantly. As we drove away, he was still standing there, watching us.

'Favell can't do anything,' Colonel Julyan told us. 'I'll soon deal with him if he comes near Manderley again. I don't think the papers will bother you any more. There may be some talk, but I'll make sure that people hear about Dr Baker.'

'Thank you very much,' Maxim said.

'What a dreadful thing illness is,' Colonel Julyan went on. 'I suppose she could not face the pain. She was such a lovely young woman, too.' Neither of us answered him.

Colonel Julyan's sister lived in London and he asked Maxim to take him to her house.

'We must thank you for all your help,' Maxim said as the magistrate got out of the car.

'I've been glad to help. You must forget it all now. Why don't you have a holiday, go abroad perhaps. Goodbye, both of you. It's been a long day.'

As Maxim started up the car, I leant back in my seat and closed my eyes. We drove on through the traffic and I felt full of peace. Nothing could hurt us any more.

We had dinner in a restaurant and Maxim phoned Frank.

'Do you think Colonel Julyan knows the truth about Rebecca's death?' I asked Maxim as we were drinking our coffee.

'Of course he knows,' Maxim said. 'But he will never say anything. I believe that Rebecca lied to me on purpose. She wanted me to kill her. That's why she laughed. She was laughing when she died.'

I did not say anything. It was all over. There was no need for Maxim to look so white and troubled.

'I'm not sure that Rebecca hasn't won, even now,' Maxim went on. 'Frank told me something rather strange on the phone. Mrs Danvers has left Manderley. There was a long-distance call for her at six. By a quarter to seven, she had gone.'

'Isn't that a good thing?' I said. 'Favell phoned her, of course. But they can't do anything to us.'

124

I was glad that Mrs Danvers had gone. Manderley could be ours. We would have people to stay. And soon, very soon Maxim and I would have children.

'Have you finished your coffee?' Maxim said to me suddenly. 'I feel that we must get back to Manderley as soon as possible. Something's wrong, I know it is.'

'But you'll be so tired,' I said.

'No, I shall be all right. We can be at Manderley by two o'clock.'

We went out to the car and Maxim covered me with a rug. It was dark now and I fell asleep almost at once. I started to dream. I saw the staircase at Manderley and Mrs Danvers standing there in her long, black dress. Then, in my dream, I was alone in the woods near Manderley. I wanted to get to the Happy Valley, but I could not find it. The dark trees were all round me. Then I was standing on the terrace. Moonlight shone on the windows. The gardens had gone and the dark woods came up to the walls of the house.

I woke up suddenly.

'You've slept for two hours,' Maxim told me. 'It's quarter past two. We shall be home by three.'

The early morning was very cold. The sky was dark now and there were no stars.

'What time did you say it was?' I said suddenly.

'It's twenty past two,' Maxim replied.

'That's strange,' I said. 'The dawn seems to be coming up over there, behind those hills. But it can't be, it's too early.'

'It's the wrong direction, too,' Maxim said 'you're looking west.'

I went on watching the sky. It was still getting lighter. A blood-red light was spreading across the sky. Maxim began to drive faster, much faster.

'That's not the dawn,' he said, 'that's Manderley.'

We reached the top of the hill. The road to Manderley lay before us. There was no moon and the sky above our heads was black. But the sky in front of us was full of dreadful light. And the light was red, red like blood. The wind blew towards us from the sea. The wind smelt of smoke and it was grey with ashes. They were the ashes of Manderley.

Points for Understanding

Note The story of Rebecca is told by a woman whose name we never know. When the narrator marries Maxim de Winter, she becomes, of course, Mrs de Winter. But this could cause some confusion since there are often references to the first Mrs de Winter who was Rebecca. For these reasons, we always refer to the story teller in the questions as the narrator.

Introduction

1 Which word in the first sentence tells us that the narrator has been to Manderley before?
2 At first in her dream, the narrator saw Manderley as beautiful as ever. What did she see when the moon shone more clearly?
3 'We would never live there free from the thoughts of the past,' said the narrator. What name was part of these thoughts of the past?
4 Where is the narrator living now?
5 Who is she living with?
6 What has happened to Manderley?

1

1 What was the narrator doing in Monte Carlo with Mrs Van Hopper?
2 'They say he's broken-hearted,' Mrs Van Hopper told the narrator.
   (a)   Who was 'he'?
   (b)   What was the name of his house?
   (c)   Why do people say he is broken-hearted?
3 'After the waiter had gone, I put the note in my pocket.'
   (a)   Who was the note from?
   (b)   What did it say?

2

1 Why did the narrator have some free time to herself?
2 'Why does Mrs Van Hopper think I'm important?' asked de Winter. What was the answer to his question?

3 'You forget that you have a home and I have none,' the narrator told de Winter. What was de Winter's reply?

4 'For the first time, I wished that I had not come.' What remark of de Winter's made the narrator feel like this?

5 Where was the secret valley?

6 Where did the narrator see Rebecca's handwriting?

7 How had Rebecca died?

3

1 How did the narrator spend her mornings when Mrs Van Hopper was in bed ill?

2 'You would not be in this car if you were like that.'
   (a) What did de Winter mean by 'like that'?
   (b) What does this remark tell us about the narrator and the way she was dressed?

3 What two things did the narrator know about de Winter?

4 Different people had called de Winter by different first names.
   (a) What did his family call him?
   (b) What had Rebecca called him?
   (c) What did de Winter want the narrator to call him?

4

1 Who decided to leave Monte Carlo and how did the narrator feel about the decision?

2 'Instead of going down to the reception desk, I ran up the stairs.'
   (a) What had the narrator been asked to do at the reception desk?
   (b) Why did she run up the stairs?

3 'Do you want a secretary?' Why did the narrator ask this question and what was de Winter's reply?

4 Why did the narrator feel she could not marry de Winter?

5 What did the narrator do to the book of poems?

5

1 'Mrs Danvers' orders, sir,' said Frith.
   (a) Who was Mrs Danvers?

(b)   What had she ordered?

(c)   Was the narrator pleased?

2 In what part of Manderley had the servants prepared rooms for the narrator and Maxim de Winter?

3 What could not be seen or heard from their rooms?

4 When had Mrs Danvers first come to Manderley?

5 Who had made all the arrangements for parties and visitors in the past?

6 Who was to make all the arrangements now?

7 What change had de Winter asked for in the choice of rooms for himself and the narrator?

8 What was the narrator thinking of when she said that Mrs Danvers might not like her at first?

9 What did the narrator think about as she sat in Rebecca's chair in the library after dinner?

6

1 How did de Winter spend his time at Manderley?

2 Who was coming to lunch?

3 How had the narrator expected the first morning at Manderley would be spent?

4 Why was the fire not lit in the library?

5 Why did the narrator not know how to find the morning-room?

6 Whose handwriting did the narrator recognize in the Guest Book?

7 'I'm afraid you have made a mistake,' the narrator said.

(a)   Who was the narrator speaking to?

(b)   Why was it not a mistake to ask for Mrs de Winter?

8 Who did the narrator think of as she sat at the writing-desk in the morning-room?

9 'It was like the writing of a schoolgirl.' Whose handwriting was the narrator speaking about?

7

1 Why did the narrator run quickly out of the morning-room?

2 What part of the house did she find herself in?

3 'It's very kind of you, Mrs Danvers,' said the narrator. 'I'll let you know.' What had Mrs Danvers offered to do?

4 Who were Beatrice and Giles and who was Frank Crawley?
5 The narrator asked: 'Is it safe to swim in the bay?' Why did everyone stop talking?
6 'Maxim had told me nothing.' What had the narrator learnt nothing about from Maxim?
7 Why did Beatrice think that Mrs Danvers must hate the narrator being at Manderley?
8 'You are not what we expected,' said Beatrice. What did Beatrice mean?

8

1 The raincoat was too big for the narrator. Why did she not have time to get another one?
2 What was meant by 'a modern young woman'?
3 Which path did the dog, Jasper, want to take?
4 What kind of scent did the flowers in the Happy Valley have?

9

1 Why did the narrator begin to climb over the rocks?
2 There was a small harbour in the other bay. What was floating in the water?
3 What was strange about the man on the shore?
4 Why did the narrator go into the cottage?
5 The strange man said: 'She doesn't go in there now. She's gone into the sea.' Who and what do you think he is speaking about?
6 How was de Winter affected by the narrator going into the bay and the cottage?
7 'The handkerchief was not mine.'
   (a) How had the handkerchief got into the narrator's pocket?
   (b) Whose handkerchief was it?
   (c) What did it smell of?

10

1 From where could the narrator hear and see the sea?
2 'I was a fool to bring you back to Manderley.' When had de Winter said these words?

3 How did the narrator think she had upset Maxim?
4 The narrator felt that the visitors were comparing her with Rebecca. What did she believe they were thinking?
5 The bishop's wife said: 'I remember her on the night of the Ball.'
   (a) What was the Ball?
   (b) Who did she remember?
   (c) How had that person looked on the night of the Ball?
6 Who did the narrator ask about the Ball? Did this person seem eager to have another Ball?
7 Who had used the cottage in the bay and what had sometimes happened on the shore?
8 What did Frank Crawley say the narrator's job was at Manderley?
9 The narrator asked Frank Crawley: 'Was Rebecca very beautiful?' What was his reply?

11

1 Who was Clarice?
2 Why did the narrator sometimes feel sorry for Mrs Danvers?
3 Why was it difficult for the narrator to forget the past?
4 How did the narrator break the china cupid? What did she do with the pieces?
5 What did Mrs Danvers think had happened to the china cupid?
6 'But you do act strangely sometimes,' de Winter said to the narrator. In what way did he think she acted strangely?
7 What remark of the narrator's made Maxim's face go dark with anger?
8 'Maxim went on staring straight in front of him.' What did the narrator believe he was thinking about?

12

1 The name of Rebecca's boat was painted on the buoy. Why did the narrator think it was a strange name?
2 Ben said: 'You're not like the other one.'
   (a) Who was the 'other one'?
   (b) What did Ben think of her eyes?
   (c) When did she come to the cottage?
   (d) Once Ben had been watching her. What had she threatened to do to Ben?

3 Who was the visitor to Manderley and who had he come to see?
4 Why did the visitor not want Maxim to know about his visit?
5 'I looked round the room, the most beautiful in Manderley.'
   (a) Whose room had it been?
   (b) Why was it strange that there was no dust and everything was clean?
   (c) What could be clearly heard from this room?
   (d) What smell did the narrator notice on the nightdress?
6 Mrs Danvers said: 'I blame myself for the accident.' What accident was she talking about?
7 What words of Mrs Danvers' made the narrator feel terribly sick?

13

1 Who was Jack Favell?
2 Why did de Winter shout in anger at Mrs Danvers?
3 What did the narrator feel life in Manderley was doing to her?

14

1 Why was Maxim not going to wear any costume at the Ball?
2 The narrator said: 'I shall wear a beautiful dress at the Ball.'
   (a) What did she tell Maxim about her costume?
   (b) What did she hope her dress at the Ball would do for her?
3 Which of the narrator's words pleased Mrs Danvers?
4 Who was Miss Caroline de Winter? Who suggested that a copy of Miss Caroline de Winter's dress should be made for the Ball?
5 Why should the narrator have to wear a wig at the Ball?

15

1 The narrator said: 'You'll both have the surprise of your lives.'
   (a) Who was she talking to?
   (b) What was the surprise going to be?
2 Why did the narrator feel so pleased on the afternoon of the Ball?
3 'I stood at the top of the stairs, smiling. I expected everyone to laugh and clap as I walked down the stairs.'
   (a) How did the others react?
   (b) What was Maxim's reaction?

4 Beatrice said: 'You could not have known.' What was it that the narrator had not known?
5 Why did the narrator remember little of the party at Manderley?

16

1 Why did the narrator think that her marriage was a failure?
2 'This was her triumph.' What was the triumph and whose was it?
3 Why did the narrator decide to speak to Mrs Danvers?
4 What were Mrs Danvers' real feelings towards the narrator?
5 How was Rebecca beaten in the end?
6 Mrs Danvers said: 'It was like a game to her.' What was like a game to Rebecca?
7 What did Mrs Danvers try to persuade the narrator to do?
8 What was the reason for the loud explosion?

17

1 Why were they going to send down a diver?
2 Captain Searle said: 'The police will have to know too.' What was it that the police would have to know?
3 Whose body was it that was lying in the boat?
4 How had Rebecca died?

18

1 Maxim said: 'It's too late.' What did he think was too late and what was the narrator's reply?
2 What were Maxim's feelings for Rebecca?
3 Why had Maxim not tried to divorce Rebecca?
4 Frank Crawley had wanted to leave Manderley, and Beatrice and Giles had stopped staying there. Why?
5 Maxim had gone down to the cottage with a gun. Who had he thought was there and why had he taken a gun with him?
6 What had Rebecca told Maxim that made him shoot her?
7 How had Maxim sunk the boat?
8 The narrator told Maxim: 'You must say that you made a mistake about the other body.' What was the other body and where was it buried?

19

1 Who was Colonel Julyan and why had he phoned?
2 'It's begun,' said Maxim. What had begun?
3 How could Mrs Danvers become dangerous?
4 What did Colonel Julyan suggest might have happened on the night that Rebecca died?
5 What had happened to the narrator in twenty-four hours?
6 What terrible word would be seen on every newspaper if the truth were known?
7 Who answered the telephone calls and met the visitors?

20

1 Tabb, the boat-builder, told the Coroner: 'There was nothing wrong with the boat when I last saw it.' What question did Tabb then ask?
2 The Coroner asked a question which made the narrator faint. What was the question?
3 'I don't trust them, Frank. They might make trouble.'
   (a) Who were they?
   (b) Where had the narrator seen them?
   (c) What kind of trouble might they make?
4 What would it mean if Frank came back to Manderley alone?

21

1 What was the verdict of the Coroner's Court?
2 Favell told Maxim: 'I've a note here that might interest you.'
   (a) Who had written the note?
   (b) Where had Favell found it?
   (c) Why had the writer wanted to speak to Favell?
   (d) Why had Favell not driven down to Manderley?
3 What did Favell want Maxim to give him?
4 What was Maxim's reply to Favell's demand?
5 What did Favell tell Colonel Julyan about Rebecca's death?

22

1 Favell thought that someone had seen de Winter murder
   Rebecca. Who was this person?
2 What did Favell say which made Maxim so angry that he
   knocked him to the floor?
3 Why do you think Ben was afraid of Favell?
4 What effect did his fear of Favell have on Ben's answers to the
   questions?
5 Colonel Julyan asked Mrs Danvers if it was true that Rebecca
   loved Favell. What was Mrs Danvers' reply?
6 Mrs Danvers said that only one thing worried Rebecca. What
   was this one thing?
7 Who had Rebecca gone to see on her last visit to London?
8 'Frank held out a small piece of paper.'
   (a)   Whose address was written on the paper?
   (b)   Why was the narrator afraid of this address?

23

1 What name had Rebecca used when she had gone to see Dr
   Baker?
2 What had Dr Baker told Rebecca?

24

1 Maxim said: 'I believe that Rebecca lied to me on purpose.'
   (a)   What lie had Rebecca told Maxim?
   (b)   What had Rebecca's purpose been in telling the lie?
2 What had Frank told Maxim on the phone?
3 On the way back to Manderley, the narrator had a dream. What
   other dream does this remind us of?
4 What had happened to Manderley?

Glossary

SECTION 1
A note on country house life

Manderley was a very large house in the country. Like many English country houses, Manderley was built with the front of the *Main Block* facing south. The two wings were at each end of the Main Block and faced east and west.

The main rooms were in the centre block. These were a large hall with a *long gallery* running round above it; the dining-room; the morning-room; and the library. The bedrooms were in the wings and the kitchens and servants' rooms were at the back of the house facing north. *The terrace* was a flat walk built above the level of the gardens and it ran round the front of the house and the outside of the west wing.

Many servants were needed to look after such a large house, to make the food and clean all the rooms. *The housekeeper* organized the work of these servants and made sure it was properly done. There were also servants who worked in the gardens and on the land belonging to the house.

There was a lot of business to be done at Manderley looking after the farms, woods and streams which belonged to the house. The person who was responsible for this work was the *agent*.

At Manderley, some things were done every day at the same time and in the same place. Meals were served in the dining-room at fixed times. After breakfast people sat in the morning-room, and after dinner they sat in the library. Tea was served in the library but, if the weather was good, tea might be served on the lawn. Sometimes food was taken out into the woods or down by the sea and the meal was called a *picnic*.

Friends of the family often came to visit in the afternoon. They did not need to be invited and when they came, they were usually asked to stay for tea. Lots of sandwiches and cakes were prepared every day for the afternoon tea.

Dinner in the evening was a special meal and visitors did not come in the evening unless they were invited. They wore evening clothes and spent the whole evening eating the meal in the dining-room and taking coffee in the library afterwards.

136

Up to the time of the Second World War, there were many houses in England like Manderley. But since the 1940s, they have become fewer and fewer. The owners of the houses which are left have, in most cases, opened them at fixed times for sightseers and tourists who pay to go into the houses and see the valuable paintings, furniture and ornaments.

agent (page 39)
see note on page 136.
Ball – *Fancy Dress Ball* (page 51)
a dance in the large hall of a big house. All the guests wear clothes which are strange and unusual.
cupid – *china cupid* (page 54)
see illustration on page 36.
corridor (page 37)
a wide passage in a house which leads from one part of the house to another.
day – *menu for the day* (page 37)
the housekeeper chose the food for lunch and dinner. Before she told the cooks to make the food, she wrote it down on paper and sent it to the mistress of the house. The mistress either approved of the menu or asked for some changes to be made.
drive (page 6)
a private road leading to the front door of a large country house.
gallery – *long gallery* (page 31)
see note on page 136.
hostess (page 76)
the wife of the owner of the house. She welcomes visitors to tea and to dinner and to parties. At a large party, she has to stand at the door and shake everybody's hand as they arrive and when they leave.
lodge (page 26)
a small house at the beginning of a drive. Servants live in the lodge and their job is to open and close the main gates.
picnic (page 53)
see note on page 136.
rug (page 35)
small, thick carpet.
rugs (page 40)
woollen coverings used to keep the legs warm or to sit on outside.

shutters (page 61)
    wooden covers for windows. Shutters can be on the inside or outside of a house.
terrace (page 50)
    see note on page 136.
window ledge (page 88)
    see illustration on page 89.
wing – *east wing* (page 29) – *west wing* (page 31)
    see note on page 136.

SECTION 2
Terms used to describe character and emotions

awful – *an awful man* (page 69)
    an unpleasant, badly behaved man.
broken-hearted (page 9)
    made extremely unhappy by the death or departure of someone who is loved deeply.
cross – *to be cross with* (page 62)
    to be angry with someone.
forward – *looking forward to* (page 72)
    to be thinking happy thoughts about something that is going to happen in the future.
get – *How do you get on with . . . ?* (page 31)
    a way of asking if you like someone.
girl – *a very modern sort of girl* (page 40)
    an expression used in the 1920s and 30s to describe a girl who wore very smart clothes and lots of make-up. It also suggests that the girl liked cigarettes, parties and dancing.
miss – *to miss someone* (page 69)
    to be unhappy because someone is away from you.
 to miss something (page 71)
  to be unable to be present at a special occasion like a party or a wedding.
yourself – *be yourself* (page 26)
    behave naturally and do not try to pretend to be different from what you are.

SECTION 3
Terms used to express strong feelings

damned (page 48)
  insulting word used to show annoyance.
do – *What's it to do with you?* (page 87)
  an insulting way of saying that it is not your business.
earth – *What on earth?* (page 43)
  an expression of surprise.
God – *Dear God* (page 55)
  an expression used to emphasize that the writer is telling the truth.
hell – *to hell with this* (page 19)
  Let's forget the complications and speak simply and honestly to
  each other.
what the hell (page 77)
  an expression of surprise and anger.
knows – *God knows* (page 109)
  a strong way of saying that you do not understand something.
sake – *for God's sake* (page 48)
  a strong way of saying 'please!'

SECTION 4
Legal terms – A note on a Coroner's Inquest

In Britain, if someone is found dead and the cause of death is not
known, a court must decide on the cause of death. The court is
called an *inquest* and the person responsible for the court is called the
coroner. Twelve local men and women are chosen to form a *jury*. The
coroner brings witnesses to the court to tell the jury what they know
about the death. The jury listens to the *evidence* of all the witnesses
and then decides on the cause of death. Their decision is read out in
court and it is known as the verdict of the court.

body – *to identify the body* (page 53)
  to look at the body of a dead person and to say who that person
  was.
coroner (page 105)
  see note above.

139

divorce (page 96)

a legal arrangement to end a marriage.

evidence (page 105)

see note on page 139.

hang (page 112)

at the time of this story, the punishment for murder in Britain was death by being hung up from a rope round the neck.

inquest (page 103)

see note on page 139.

magistrate – *the local magistrate* (page 101)

the man who makes decisions about law cases in a court in a country district. He always sends important law cases to higher courts in a town or city.

sentence (page 113)

to read out in court the punishment that a criminal is to be given.

verdict (page 109)

see note on page 139.

SECTION 5

Terms to do with ships and the sea

bay (page 39)

a sheltered place formed by a curve in the coast. See illustration on page 92.

beach (page 45)

the piece of ground where the land meets the sea. See illustration on page 47.

break up (page 91)

destroyed by the movement of the waves and the sea.

buoy (page 46)

something which floats in the water and is fixed to the bottom of the sea by rope or by chain. When a boat is near the coast, it can be fixed to the buoy.

cabin (page 93)

a room in a boat or a ship.

coastguard (page 91)

someone who watches the sea near the coast and looks out for ships in trouble.

dinghy (page 98)
   a small boat.
diver (page 91)
   a man who goes down under the sea wearing special clothing which
   allows him to stay under the water for some time.
harbour (page 46)
   a sheltered place where boats can be tied up to the wall or to buoys.
   See the illustration on page 47.
harbour-master (page 93)
   the man in charge of a harbour.
rockets (page 88)
   a ship in trouble sends up rockets to ask for help. The rockets make
   a loud noise and cause a bright light.
sea-cocks (page 98)
   a boat which has a wash-basin and a toilet must have a system
   which lets dirty water run out of the boat into the sea. The job of
   the sea-cocks is to let the dirty water out, but to prevent the sea
   water from coming in.
tide (page 45)
   the movements of the earth and the moon cause the water in the
   seas and the oceans to move towards the land and then away from
   it. This movement of sea water is called the tide.

SECTION 6
General

ache – *my legs ached* (page 48)
   my legs were tired and painful.
awkward (page 8)
   not knowing how to move one's arms and legs gracefully.
bank (page 43)
   a sloping piece of ground usually covered with grass.
bishop (page 51)
   a priest who is in charge of other priests in a particular area.
Bond Street (page 73)
   a street of shops in London where very expensive clothes are sold.

bride (page 30)

a woman who is about to be married or has only been married for a short time.

cloud – *a cloud of dark hair* (page 52)

her hair formed a soft shape round her head.

copy (page 73)

to make something exactly like something else.

costumes (page 72)

unusual clothes worn for a party.

draw – *the curtains were drawn* (page 31)

to pull curtains together across a window.

files (page 121)

containers for keeping papers and documents in good order.

fitting – *tightly fitting* (page 76)

clothes worn close to the body. See illustration on page 78.

gossip (page 11)

unpleasant talk about people and what they are doing.

label (page 35)

to put a piece of paper on a container saying what is inside.

late – *the late Mrs de Winter* (page 31)

late is used as an adjective in this way to refer to someone who is dead.

pat – *a pat on the head* (page 50)

to touch a dog's head with your hand to show that you are pleased with it.

propose (page 23)

to ask someone to marry you.

shell – *an empty shell* (page 7)

the walls of a ruined house which has been destroyed.

triumph (page 85)

a moment of joy, success and victory.

victim (page 8)

someone to whom something unpleasant happens.

wig (page 75)

false hair worn by someone to make them look more handsome. See illustration on page 78.

winding (page 6)

turning and twisting.

Of Mice and Men *by John Steinbeck*
Bleak House *by Charles Dickens*
The Great Ponds *by Elechi Amadi*
Rebecca *by Daphne du Maurier*
Our Mutual Friend *by Charles Dickens*
The Grapes of Wrath *by John Steinbeck*
The Return of the Native *by Thomas Hardy*
Weep Not, Child *by Nugugi wa Thiong'o*
Precious Bane *by Mary Webb*
Mine Boy *by Peter Abrahams*

For further information on the full selection of
Readers at all five levels in the series, please refer
to the Macmillan Readers catalogue.

Published by Macmillan Heinemann ELT
Between Towns Road, Oxford OX4 3PP
Macmillan Heinemann ELT is an imprint of
Macmillan Publishers Limited
Companies and representatives throughout the world

ISBN 0 435 27261 6

© *Rebecca* Daphne du Maurier 1938
First published by Victor Gollancz Ltd 1938
This retold version by Margaret Tarner for Macmillan Guided Readers

Text © Margaret Tarner 1977, 1992, 1998, 2002
First published 1977. Reissued 1992
Design and illustration © Macmillan Publishers Limited 1998, 2002
This version first published 2002

Illustrated by Anthony Colbert

Cover shows detail from 'Summertime, Cornwall' by Dame Laura Knight
(Reproduced by permission of Curtis Brown Group Ltd)
Cover design by Threefold Design

Printed in China

2005 2004 2003
23 22 21 20 19 18 17